Classical Theism and Buddhism

Also available from Bloomsbury

Debating Christian Religious Epistemology,
edited by John M. DePoe and Tyler Dalton McNabb
Differences in Identity in Philosophy and Religion,
edited by Lydia Azadpour, Sarah Flavel and Russell Re Manning
Nonexistent Objects in Buddhist Philosophy,
by Zhihua Yao
Faith and Reason in Continental and Japanese Philosophy,
by Takeshi Morisato
Comparative Philosophy without Borders,
edited by Arindam Chakrabarti and Ralph Weber

Classical Theism and Buddhism

Connecting Metaphysical and Ethical Systems

Tyler Dalton McNabb and Erik Baldwin

BLOOMSBURY ACADEMIC
LONDON • NEW YORK • OXFORD • NEW DELHI • SYDNEY

BLOOMSBURY ACADEMIC
Bloomsbury Publishing Plc
50 Bedford Square, London, WC1B 3DP, UK
1385 Broadway, New York, NY 10018, USA
29 Earlsfort Terrace, Dublin 2, Ireland

BLOOMSBURY, BLOOMSBURY ACADEMIC and the Diana logo
are trademarks of Bloomsbury Publishing Plc

First published in Great Britain 2022

Cover image: Kun lam goddess in Saint Francois-Xavier chapel in Coloane.
Photo by: Godong/Universal Images Group via Getty Images.

A catalogue record for this book is available from the British Library.

Library of Congress Cataloging-in-Publication Data
Names: McNabb, Tyler Dalton, author. | Baldwin, Erik Daniel, author.
Title: Classical theism and Buddhism: connecting metaphysical and ethical systems /
Tyler Dalton McNabb and Erik Baldwin.
Description: 1. | New York: Bloomsbury Academic, 2022. |
Includes bibliographical references and index.
Identifiers: LCCN 2021035904 (print) | LCCN 2021035905 (ebook) |
ISBN 9781350189133 (hardback) | ISBN 9781350189140 (pdf) |
ISBN 9781350189157 (ebook)
Subjects: LCSH: Theism–Comparative studies. | Buddhism–Relations–Theism.
Classification: LCC BL200 .M365 2022 (print) |
LCC BL200 (ebook) | DDC 294.3/4211–dc23
LC record available at https://lccn.loc.gov/2021035904
LC ebook record available at https://lccn.loc.gov/2021035905

ISBN:	HB:	978-1-3501-8913-3
	ePDF:	978-1-3501-8914-0
	eBook:	978-1-3501-8915-7

Typeset by Integra Software Services Pvt. Ltd.

To find out more about our authors and books visit www.bloomsbury.com
and sign up for our newsletters.

I, Tyler, dedicate this book to my wife (Priscilla), my children (Eden, Elijah, Ezra, Eva-Maria, and Ezekiel), and to my friend, Xuan Zhao. May the God of Classical Theism grant all of you many years.

I, Erik, dedicate this book my wife, Melanie, and to our daughter, Naomi. Lord, protect and watch over our family.

Contents

Acknowledgments

First, we want to thank those who have informed our views about Classical Theism and about Buddhism. Tyler specifically would like to thank Victoria Harrison, Rhett Gayle, and Xuan Zhao. Erik would like to specifically thank Donald Mitchell and Bradley Hawkins.

Second, we'd like to acknowledge our families. They have allowed us to work on this project, and thus, they have sacrificed time that could have been spent with us.

Finally, we want to thank *Perichoresis* for allowing us to use the following work: Tyler Dalton McNabb and Joseph Blado, "Mary and Fátima: A Modest C-Inductive Argument for Catholicism," *Perichoresis* 18/5 (2020), 55–65. We also want to thank *The Heythrop Journal* for allowing us to use a section from Tyler Dalton McNabb and Michael DeVito, "Has Oppy Done Away with the Aristotelian Proof?" *Heythrop Journal* 61/5 (2020), 723–31. And of course, we want to thank Joseph Blado and Michael DeVito for allowing us to incorporate some of the aforementioned work in our volume.

Introduction: Context, Outline, and Motivation

Paul Williams, an expert in Mahayana Buddhism, was a practicing Buddhist for most of his adult life. This, however, changed when he began to seek answers to questions about his moral experience and to questions such as why there is something rather than nothing.[1] Williams found that Christianity offered more satisfactory answers than Buddhism and thus converted to Catholicism. Williams is very clear in his autobiography that he sees Buddhism as an atheistic religious tradition, one that is incompatible with Christianity.

In *Plantingian Religious Epistemology and World Religions: Problems and Prospects*,[2] we defended a view similar to Williams. Specifically, we argued that theism is incompatible with Buddhism. Our purposes in that volume pertained to whether different religious traditions could utilize Alvin Plantinga's religious epistemology. One of the key indicators whether a religious tradition could utilize Plantinga's epistemology is that it espoused a form of theism. There is tension between a tradition that advocates that ultimate reality is something like a personal God and a tradition, like certain Buddhist traditions, that argues that ultimate reality is *śūnyatā*, "empty of own-being," i.e., lacking independent or unconditioned existence. Given that the prospects of theism on Buddhism seemed unfavorable, we argued (in Chapter Seven) that a Mahayana Buddhist could not utilize Plantingian religious epistemology.

David Burton, in *Buddhism: A Contemporary Philosophical Investigation*, recognizes that when people hear of the idea of a Buddhist Christian, those who are sufficiently knowledgeable of both Buddhism and Christianity tend to think such a person will have engaged these religious traditions only superficially. How could one fully familiar with the core doctrines of both Buddhism and Christianity think that *both* sets of doctrines were true? Discussing the incompatibility of Buddhism and Christianity, Burton states the following:

> Christians believe in a creator God whereas Buddhists do not. Most Christians regard Jesus as uniquely salvific whereas Buddhists do not share this conviction. The Buddhist soteriological aim is nirvana, which seems very different from the Christian conception of heaven. Buddhists usually believe in Karma and rebirth whereas Christians normally do not, and so on.[3]

Burton isn't convinced, however, that this necessarily needs to be the case. Burton seems open to the idea that one could identify as a Buddhist Christian, by which he means one who sees that these religious traditions are incompatible but nonetheless continues to identify as both a Buddhist and as a Christian. Burton recognizes that the divided loyalties could create a "psychologically (and socially) uncomfortable identity to maintain."[4] The Buddhist Christian, of course, could remain agnostic as to whether the Christian story or the Buddhist story is true. Perhaps she feels psychologically comforted to live out both lives to give her the best shot at getting to heaven or reaching nirvana. This could always backfire however; that is, it could be that because she didn't choose one particular religion that she loses her spot in heaven or disqualifies herself from realizing nirvana. Burton opens the door, however, to the possibility that, "the apparent contradictions can be overcome or are not as serious or fundamental as they may first appear." He goes on to suggest that "the strategies for accomplishing this harmonization are varied."[5] It is worthwhile to consider a few accounts of the nature and possibility of double religious belonging before saying more about the project of this book.

Jay McDaniel suggests three metaphors that can help us to unpack the notion of double religious belonging. One metaphor is to imagine people crossing a bridge, such as when one crosses over into the world of Buddhism to gain some insight to take back to the world of Christianity. Another is to imagine people hooked up to intravenous tubes that provide one with fluid from the Christian and Buddhist lineages for the sake of living a more complete life. The third is to imagine people whose primary roots are in Christian (Buddhist) soil that have secondary roots in Buddhist (Christian) soil and as such are anchored in and are sustained by both Christian and Buddhist soil.[6] Taking a process approach to double religious belonging, McDaniel argues that because, ideally, double religious belongings avoid defensiveness and welcome learning from other religions, we should unpack double religious belonging as "analogous to a tree with two strong roots, one primary and the other secondary."[7]

Ruben L. F. Habito, a contemplative ex-Jesuit, follower of the spiritual exercises of St. Ignatius and a Zen practitioner of the Sanbo Kyodan lineage, testifies to having had both the Zen Buddhist experience of *Kensho* (seeing one's true nature, that is, one's Buddha nature) and the experience of *Contemplatio ad Amorem* (contemplation of God's love). He finds an experiential and conceptual convergence in the Christian practice of *metanoia*, the process of transformation of one's mind and heart and of one's entire mode of being, and the Buddhist practice of the personalization of enlightenment, "the embodiment of the awakened way," which involves a radical change in one's daily life and one's entire mode of being.[8] He also finds convergence in the Catholic figure of Mary, the mother of Jesus, and the Buddhist figure of Bodhisattva Kanzeon, the Japanese name for the Chinese Goddess of mercy and compassion, the subject of the Heart Sutra and the Kanzeon Sutra.[9] In *Healing Breath: Zen for Christians and Buddhists in a Wounded World*, Habito considers the possibility of a Christian also being devoted to taking up the path of Zen "as a way of living the Christian spiritual life."[10]

Catherine Cornille suggests that, in the context of interreligious dialogue at the level of practice, double religious belonging is possible "when one remains within the sphere of compatible or complementary beliefs and practices."[11] She notes that the selective adoption of beliefs and practices, such as a Christian's embrace of certain aspects of the Buddhist analysis of suffering and how to overcome it, does not constitute double religious belonging. She points out that for those who would attempt to adopt more than one religion, their fundamental religious beliefs will come into conflict, leading one to accept the primacy of one religion over the other. She suggests that double religious belonging is a sort of intermediate step, a temporary stage or transition from accepting the full authority and primacy of one religion to that of another, or as a kind of individualistic integration of the two traditions.[12]

There are different takes on the issue and possibility of double religious belonging, and there are different ways to understand Burton's claim that one can identify as both a Buddhist and as a Christian. There are reasons why some Buddhists and Christians care about double religious belonging and so choose to take up more than one religious tradition, at both the theoretical level and at the level of practice. Without committing ourselves to one way of unpacking the notion of double religious belonging, this book is an attempt to resolve the apparent contradictions derived by the affirmation of both the core beliefs of Buddhism and Classical Theism.

Notice that the Classical Theism label used is much broader than simply discussing how core Buddhist beliefs can be compatible with core Christian beliefs. The sort of theism we discuss for *most* of this volume is compatible with the main religious traditions associated with the figure in the Torah known as Abraham. As such, our project is appropriately broad so as to include various versions of theism, including Judaism, Christianity, and Islam, as well as, by extension, non-Abrahamic monotheisms, such as Dvaita Vedanta and Sikhism, that are sufficiently similar to Abrahamic monotheism. However, while most of this volume is dedicated to discussing Classical Theism and its compatibility with Buddhism, in the last two chapters, we do specifically address claims made by Christians and discuss their relevance in responding to pluralist objections developed by John Hick. Nonetheless, for most of this volume, we plan to explicate the theistic doctrines that comfortably fit under a larger umbrella that includes core beliefs of Christianity, Islam, and Judaism. If we can show that the Abrahamic conception of God is compatible with Buddhism, we will have established something important. This book, then, could be seen as making a qualified statement from our previous work with respect to whether Buddhism can be conjoined with certain forms of theism.

In Chapter One, we engage with what we take to be the essential metaphysical doctrines of Buddhism and the essential metaphysical doctrines of Classical Theism. After we explicate these doctrines, we argue that there isn't a contradiction between core Buddhist doctrines and Classical Theist doctrines. Of course, there is a long-standing critique of theism within the Buddhist tradition. In Chapter Two, we engage these objections and argue that they fail to undermine our project. However, while one might find the Buddhist-styled objections to Classical Theism to be unsound, nonetheless, one could still be worried about contemporary objections to Classical Theism which might render our project incoherent. This is why, in Chapter Three, we survey various contemporary objections and find them wanting. Since the arguments in Chapters One, Two, and Three will be based primarily on Classical Theism (in contrast with what is at times called Neo-Classical Theism or Theistic Personalism),[13] we think this section could be of interest to anyone who is interested in the metaphysics of Theism. While important to our project, this section stands alone.

In the second section of this book, we engage the ethics and soteriology of Buddhism and what we will refer to as the Abrahamic traditions. Specifically, in Chapter Four, we first explicate the ethics of Buddhism. We then will examine popular theories in the theistic ethics literature. We argue that while ethics construed in the theistic traditions appears *prima facie* at odds with the ethics described in the Buddhist literature, there is a clear way to synthesize the relevant ethical traditions. Similarly, in Chapter Five, we survey the various soteriological systems as expressed within each of the Abrahamic traditions. We take what we believe to be the fundamental soteriological doctrines from these traditions and synthesize them with what we call Mere Buddhist Soteriology. By "synthesize" we don't mean to suggest the Hegelian view that although Buddhist doctrines and Christian doctrines are antithetical it is possible to dialectically combine them so as to derive a new, higher body of truth. Nor do we mean to take a certain subset of Buddhist doctrines and certain subset of Christian doctrines and use that as basis to formulate a new religious tradition. Rather, we mean to show that it's possible for someone to affirm the core doctrines of both traditions in a coherent or holistic manner.

Finally, in the last section, we look at how a Classical Theist should understand Buddhist religious experience. In Chapter Six, we take a look at John Hick's understanding of religious experience. Specifically, we engage with his argument for religious pluralism. While we go on to reject Hick's pluralism, in our final chapter, Chapter Seven, we argue that the Classical Theist can still take the Buddhist's religious experience, specifically the experience of emptiness (*śūnyatā*), as veridical, without denying any core doctrine of Classical Theism.

Before we do all of this, however, we first provide brief motivations as to why someone might be inclined to identify as a Buddhist Classical Theist. It is important to note that we don't intend thoroughly to argue that the following motivations are compelling or are sufficient reasons to identify as a Buddhist Classical Theist. In fact, we personally do not affirm the metaphysics involved in Buddhism. We are merely giving a brief sketch to explain why someone might be interested in identifying as a Buddhist Classical Theist in order to provide some practical context for our overall project.

Motivation for Classical Theism

In *Summa Theologica* (Part 1, Question 2, Article 2), Thomas Aquinas argues from motion to the existence of God. Specifically, he utilizes Aristotle's principle that "everything that is in motion must be moved by something else."[14] In contemporary technical terms, Edward Feser, explicating Aquinas's version of the principle, renders the principle thus: "any potency that is being actualized is being actualized by something else (and in particular by something that is already actual)."[15] We can look all around and see that change occurs. We see changes in substances, such as when ice turns into water and water turns into steam. We see local change, such as when someone throws a box off a balcony and the box falls and hits the ground. We also see change with respect to the quantity of a thing. For example, we can see a large chocolate bar broken up into many smaller pieces.

There are at least two necessary conditions for change to occur. First, there has to be the potential to change. Second, there must be an external cause which moves the potential for change into actual change. For example, say that a person holding a stick pushes a rock with the stick and the rock moves and crushes a can of soda.[16] The stick has the potential to be picked up and it has the potential to move the rock. The rock has the potential to be moved by the stick to crush the can. And the can has the potential to be crushed. (We can understand, for the sake of the example, the movement of an arm to be an uncaused cause, though it's possible to continue to explain why a hand is able to pick up the stick in further terms.) The objects in the scenario derive their causal power from the arm that is in motion.

Aquinas argues, however, that you can't explain change by postulating an infinite number of derivative or secondary causes. For example, imagine that there is an infinite number of train cars, and each train car is connected with another train car. However, now imagine that there is no engine. Could the train cars move at all? Even if you can postulate more train cars, you won't be able to explain why there is motion with respect to any of the cars unless you postulate an engine. Or, going back to the example of the stick, you can postulate an infinite amount of additional derivative causes, but you won't be able to make sense of movement if you take out the primary cause (i.e., the arm). In the same way, Aquinas argues that unless you postulate an uncaused caused, that is, something that lacks potentiality and is strictly speaking Pure Act, you won't be able to make sense of the change that we perceive in our basic human experience. Aquinas takes this Pure Act to be the God of Classical Theism.[17]

Now, it might be said that Aquinas's argument is arcane and intellectually outdated. Perhaps one thinks that Newton's First Law, or the Law of Inertia, which states that, "Every body perseveres in its state of rest, or of uniform motion in a right line, unless it is compelled to change that state by forces impressed thereon,"[18] disproves Aquinas's argument. Appealing to this law, one might object that once an object is caused to move it no longer needs to be caused to move. If this is so, then after you explain why motion began, you don't need to explain why an object continues to move in the way that it does. It doesn't need a cause at all. That this is so is supposed to undermine Aquinas's First Way.

This objection fails to be a good response for several reasons. First, the Law of Inertia only applies to local motion. As explained above, Aquinas had a much larger understanding of motion. Even if you didn't require an unmoved mover to explain local motion, you would still need an unmoved mover to explain change that happens when one substance changes into another substance or when the quality of an object changes.[19] Second, you would still need to explain why anything started to move at all. Finally, as Feser points out, we are left with "the question of what actualizes the potential existence of things having natures of the sort described by the principle of inertia, and that to answer this question we have (for reasons already seen) to appeal to something which is pure act."[20]

Graham Oppy seems to take the objection from the Law of Inertia a step forward in endorsing what is known as Existential Inertia (EI). Oppy suggests that any object which has the potential to exist in the way that it currently exists doesn't need an explanation for as to why it continues to exist in the way that it currently exists.[21] All that's required to explain why it continues to exist in the way that it does is that no other object intervenes and moves the object such that some other potential it possesses is turned into act. Oppy gives the following thought experiment:

> Yesterday, throughout the entire day, there was a red chair in my room. Pick some time t around noon yesterday. At t, the chair existed, and the chair was red. Moreover, at t, the chair had the potential to exist, and to be red, at $t + \varepsilon$, where ε is some relatively short time interval (say, a millionth of second). Do we need to postulate the existence of some distinct thing that exists through $(t, t + \varepsilon)$ that actualizes at $t+\varepsilon$ the potential that the chair had at t to both exist and be red at $t+\varepsilon$? I do not think so. Given that, at t, the chair has the potential to exist and to be red at $t + \varepsilon$, all that is required for the realization of this potential is that nothing intervenes to bring it about, either that the chair does not exist, or that the chair is not red, at $t + \varepsilon$. Potentials to remain unchanged do not require distinct actualizers; all they require is the absence of any preventers of the actualization of those potentials. In particular, things that have the potential to go on existing go on existing unless there are preventers—internal or external—that cause those things to cease to exist.[22]

Feser directly responds to Oppy's objection in a recent debate. Feser points out that in order for the chair to remain red at t + ε, the chemical microstructure of the chair will have to continue being in a certain way.[23] That is, if the microchemical structure of the chair were different, the chair's potential to be red wouldn't be actualized. This seems to refute the idea that the red chair can remain red at t + ε as long as no other object intervenes. Rather, as Feser puts it, in order for the chair to retain its redness, something outside of its redness needs to be in place,[24] namely the microchemical structure. Setting aside the debate about the soundness of these arguments, one who is convinced by Aquinas's First Way will have sufficient motivation to affirm Aquinas's Classical Theism.[25] But, why might someone also be motivated to endorse Buddhism?

Motivation for Buddhism

As mentioned in the previous section, change is part of our basic human experience. Change, however, can give rise to great anxiety. Not knowing what tomorrow might bring may lead one to seek helpful coping mechanisms. As we explicate in detail in the first chapter, Buddhists believe that entities are ultimately empty. That is, entities don't exist as ontologically or causally independent from one another. Rather, all entities depend on other entities for their existence. A divorced man can take solace in the fact that he is still connected to what he understands to be his wife. The child who mourns being abandoned by her father can rest quietly knowing that her father is still in some sense a part of her life. There is a sense that all of reality is part of one organic whole. Coming to this realization will inevitably relieve at least some anxiety.

Buddhists also endorse the impermanence thesis—that all things only exist from moment to moment. Buddhists hold that coming to believe that what one experiences is actually empty leads to detachment from suffering. According to Buddhism, if one becomes detached from the entities that one experiences, one will no longer find change to be problematic. There isn't some entity that one must have in order to be happy, such as a new house or a spouse. Entities lack an independent nature and only exist momentarily. As we will discuss in more detail in the next chapter, as soon as S desires X, both S and X no longer can be said to exist.

Not only might one be attracted to Buddhist philosophy as a means to alleviate anxiety and depression, but one might simply find the metaphysics of Buddhism plausible. That is, one might see Buddhist philosophy as a natural entailment from the basic metaphysics it endorses. We will engage with reasons why someone might be attracted to Buddhist metaphysics in Chapter One. For now, it's simply important to explain why a person who is attracted to Classical Theism might also be inclined to endorse core tenets found in Buddhism. We turn to argue that the "Buddhist Classical Theist" can have their metaphysical cake and eat it too.

1

Can a Buddhist Be a Classical Theist?

C. S. Lewis famously used the term "Mere Christianity" to refer to the fundamentals of the Christian faith that could be agreed upon by Christians of all stripes.[1] Following Lewis, we will use the phrase "Mere Buddhism" to refer to the core tenets of Buddhism that can generally be agreed on by most Buddhists. Jay Garfield summarizes the core tenets of Buddhism as follows:

> Suffering (*dukkha*) or discontent is ubiquitous in the world ...
>
> The origin of dukkha is in primal confusion about the fundamental nature of reality, and so its cure is at bottom a reorientation toward ontology and an awakening (*bodhi*) to the actual nature of existence.
>
> All phenomena are impermanent (*anitya*), interdependent (*pratītya-samutpāda*) and have no intrinsic nature (*śūnya*) ...
>
> Fundamental confusion is to take phenomena, including preeminently oneself, to be permanent, independent and to have an essence or intrinsic nature (*svabhāva*).
>
> The elimination (*nirvāṇa*), or at least the substantial reduction of dukkha through such reorientation, is possible.
>
> An ethically appropriate orientation toward the world is characterized by the cultivation of *mudita* (an attitude of rejoicing in the welfare and goodness of others, of *mettā*) beneficence toward others, and especially of *karuṇā* (commitment to act for the welfare of sentient beings).[2]

While there is much to be said about how these tenets are compatible with theistic belief, especially with the Abrahamic traditions, the central metaphysical claim that "All phenomena are impermanent (*anitya*), interdependent (*pratītya-samutpāda*) and have no intrinsic nature (*śūnya*)" seems to be what is most relevant for determining whether a Mere Buddhist can be a Classical Theist. Call these fundamental metaphysical doctrines FMD for short.

In this chapter, we will argue that Classical Theism is compatible with FMD, at least, FMD according to Garfield. In addition to this, we will resolve apparent conflicts between Buddhist philosophy and other doctrines that Classical Theists will want to preserve. However, in order to do any of this, we will first need to unpack FMD. We then will clarify what we mean by Classical Theism. This will finally lead us to argue that FMD is compatible with Classical Theism.

Interdependence, Impermanence, and Emptiness

The standard formulation of the doctrine of dependent origination goes as follows: "When this arises, that arises; when this does not occur, that does not occur."[3] David Burton summarizes the doctrine by stating that, "all entities have a dependently arisen and conceptually constructed existence ...."[4] Jan Westerhoff describes the dependence thesis in terms of existential dependence. He defines the dependence thesis in the following way: "An object *a* existentially depends on objects falling under the property F iff necessarily, if *a* exists there exists something falling under F."[5] The doctrine, however, can be understood even more precisely.

Dependent origination can be broken up into three parts.[6] First, there is causal dependency. As Garfield puts it, "All events in time, all Buddhist philosophers agree, occur in dependence to prior causes and conditions, and all states of affairs cease when the cause and conditions that are necessary for their occurrence cease."[7] When someone asks, "what caused a tree to grow in the garden?" there are prior conditions that one can appeal to in response. For example, there was a seed that was put into the soil and the seed was watered. There being a seed in the soil also relies on prior causes. Those causes rely on other causes. In like manner, all states of affairs are causally interdependent.

Second, there is part–whole or mereological dependence. Composite entities are dependent on their parts for their existence and the properties that they exemplify.[8] Finally, there is a conceptual dependence. The things that exist at a phenomenological or conventional level depend on minds for their existence.[9] While there are various different approaches to understanding what one means by conceptual experience, we needn't get bogged down in the details. For our purposes, the brief sketch above is sufficient to understand what we mean by the doctrine of dependent origination, what we will now refer to as the interdependence thesis for sake of clarity and accessibility.

The interdependence thesis is usually conjoined with the impermanence thesis. Roughly, the impermanence thesis endorses that all things exist only momentarily. In order to clarify reasoning in favor of this thesis, it's important to clarify the different types of change that are discussed in the literature on Buddhist metaphysics. Something can change in both a gross and subtle way. By affirming that something changes in a gross sense, one merely affirms that the thing changes over time. For example, a baby human turns into an adult human being. This sort of change entails subtle change. Subtle change is the change that occurs from moment to moment. At one moment, S possesses the property of being 259,104 hours old and soon S will lose that property and gain the property of being 259,105 hours old. Buddhist philosophers deny that a thing can experience subtle change while keeping its identity intact. Motivating this view is a radical interpretation of the Law of Identity, where any small difference between A and B makes it such that A and B are not identical.[10]

Interdependence and impermanence are supposed to lead to the doctrine of emptiness. There are various ways to understand emptiness. Nāgārjuna perhaps has the most well-known approach to understanding emptiness. Nāgārjuna argues that things at the ultimate layer of existence lack *svabhāva*.[11] *Svabhāva* is often translated as inherent existence or own being.[12] It can be more precisely defined as an entity having existence independently of anything else, including conceptual constructions.[13]

Nāgārjuna argued that the doctrine of emptiness is necessitated by the interdependence thesis. In the context of why *dharmas*, purportedly fundamentally existent entities roughly analogous to atoms, can't possess *svabhāva* given the principle of interdependence, Garfield explains:

> To have svabhāva in the sense relevant to Madhyamaka is to have one's nature intrinsically, as the Abhidharmika believe that dharams have their natures. But Madhyamikas argued that to exist in this way would also require being independent. For if a dharma is caused by, or is the cause of, another dharma, as they must be, given the doctrine of dependent origination, then part of what it is to be a particular dharma is to be caused by particular predecessors, to cause successors, to be part of certain composites, and so on. That is, since it is of the very nature of all phenomena, including putatively fundamental dharmas, to be interdependent, then no identity conditions can be given for any phenomenon independent of others. So, since all phenomena are interdependent, and svabhāva requires independence, svabhāva is impossible, a property nothing can have.[14]

Similarly, impermanence makes it impossible for things to possess identity over time. Every thing ceases to exist as soon as it comes into being. It's even difficult to talk about a specific "thing" existing, because prior to talking about it as an existing thing, the purported object has undergone change, and hence no longer is (at least not is as it was prior to linguistic conceptualization and description).

While Nāgārjuna's understanding of emptiness isn't affirmed by all Buddhists (for example, the *Abhidharaa* tradition affirms that dharmas are not empty of being), Nāgārjuna's view is widely held. Nāgārjuna's understanding of emptiness is robust. In addition to thinking that all things lack *svabhāva*, Nāgārjuna thought that there was nothing behind emptiness. For Nāgārjuna, even emptiness was empty. We don't plan to synthesize this specific view with Classical Theism. Rather, when we refer to Nāgārjuna's view of emptiness, we have in mind the view that emptiness applies to all things. If we can show that this understanding of Nāgārjuna's notion of emptiness—the view that emptiness applies to all things—is compatible with Classical Theism, then other versions of Buddhism are also likely to be compatible with Classical Theism, too. Having now explicated FMD, we will now move to explicating what we mean by Classical Theism.

Classical Theism

Classical Theism is, roughly, the thesis that God exists and that God is strongly immutable, impassible, and metaphysically simple. We will now proceed by explicating each term in turn. The philosophical literature makes a distinction between weak immutability and strong immutability. Weak immutability is in reference to God's character not changing while strong immutability is in reference to God being wholly unchanging.[15] On the latter view, God does not gain or lose properties, with the possible exception of relational properties, also known as "Cambridge" properties. For example, Xanthippe has the property *being a wife* before Socrates drinks the hemlock. After Socrates drinks it, she loses that property and acquires the property *being a widow*. Xanthippe's "change" depends entirely on standing in certain contingent relations to Socrates, factors that are external to her intrinsic nature. Similarly, if God gains or loses relational or external properties, that wouldn't bring about actual change in God's nature.

The doctrine of immutability helps motivate the doctrine of impassibility, the thesis that God is not affected by external forces. Since God is wholly immutable, God can't be affected by anyone or anything. God might have passions, but He has experienced all of His emotions simultaneously for all eternity.

While immutability and impassibility are closely connected, these attributes are not as clearly connected with God's simplicity. The doctrine of divine simplicity is, roughly, the thesis that God lacks parts. Most Classical Theists deny that God possesses various properties, at least, in a strict sense. Classical Theists recognize that God cannot depend on the existence of those properties because then it would follow that those properties would be more fundamental than God. One line of reasoning for this is as follows. To suppose that God has parts is to introduce a distinction between the being of God and the nature of God. If we understand God's nature in terms of the essential properties God must have in order to be God, then making a distinction between God's being and God's nature in turn presupposes that those properties (the ones God must have in order to exist) exist, in some sense, prior to or independently of God's being. This, of course, goes against God being *a se*, and this would be a conclusion that Perfect Being theologians would want to avoid.

The Classical Theist denies that we can understand God's attributes in a univocal sense. Classical Theists deny that God and humans are univocally good, good in the same exact sense, and they deny that God and humans are good in completely different, or equivocal, senses. They affirm that while the goodness of God and the goodness of humans are different, there is an analogical sense in which the goodness of God and the goodness of humans overlap. And this is the case with all of God's attributes, not just God's goodness. Classical Theists then, refer to language about God as being analogical.

For the Classical Theist, not only is it proper to say that God's existence and essence are identical, but it would be proper to say that

God's power is identical to His goodness and His goodness is identical to all of His other predicates. Clearly, on this picture, it wouldn't make sense to understand God's power or God's goodness univocally. Again, in God, not only are power and goodness identical to each other, but God is identical to His power and to His goodness. William Vallicella, using properties in a loose sense, states, "It is not just that God has properties no creature has; the properties he has he has in a way different from the way any creature has any of its properties. God has his properties by being them."[16]

At this juncture, one might raise the objection that if God has His properties by being them, then that makes God out to be a property. For instance, Alvin Plantinga writes:

> [I]f God is identical with each of his properties, then each of his properties is identical with each of his properties, so that God has but one property ... if God is identical with each of his properties, then, since each of his properties is a property, he is a property ... Accordingly God has just one property: himself ... [but] if God is a property, then he isn't a person but a mere abstract object.[17]

Responding to Plantinga's objection, John Lamont argues that Aquinas would deny that if God is a property, then God is an abstract object. According to Aquinas, properties are not abstract objects, for there are no abstract objects. Rather, he maintains that all existent things are actual, having a location in space and time.[18] (Note again that God is not a thing that exists in space and time but is existence itself.) Moreover, God's nature is not an abstract or immaterial individualized form, for matter is that which individuates form, and God is not material.[19] Lamont argues:

> The properties that we attribute to the divine nature are not like determinates that admit of no further determination. There are many different kinds of power, wisdom, goodness, beauty. Even in created things there are forms of one of these properties that are

also forms of another; being a good painting is the same as being a beautiful painting, for example, although being a good X is not the same as being a beautiful X. Thus it is quite possible to suppose that there is a property that falls under all these different general properties that we attribute to God, and is the highest form of every one of these properties. We have no idea what such a property would be like—as Aquinas is the first to point out—but that is no reason to suppose that it does not exist.[20]

On Aquinas's view, we can truthfully ascribe to God's properties in their literal albeit analogical sense because these property ascriptions are general in nature. Moreover, ascribing a property to God (e.g., God is good) is really a kind of shorthand way of saying that God is identical to his goodness. As Etienne Gilson writes:

> In the case of God, every judgment, even if it takes the forms of a judgment of attribution, is really a judgment of existence. Whether one speaks of His Essence or His Substance or His Goodness or His wisdom, one only repeats—He is *esse*.[21] [That is, God is his own act-of-being, *ipsum esse*; He is not an *ens*, a thing that has existence.][22]

And while these property ascriptions are literally true, we don't know "the determinate form they take in the divine nature," which is compatible with Aquinas's view that we can't comprehend and indeed are ignorant of God's nature.[23]

In light of the above arguments, we maintain that the Classical Theist is correct to ascribe or attribute properties to God, at least in a loose sense, and that doing so is in accord with Aquinas's view that God is metaphysically simple. However, in a strict or technical sense, it would be incorrect to say that God *possesses* or *has* properties, for that would make God out to be just another existing thing. God isn't merely a being. He isn't something that has or possesses being. God isn't just another thing that happens to exist or happens to be a part of reality. Rather, God is Existence; God is ultimate reality. Brain Davis puts it as follows:

> If God accounts for the world at all ... then God is (a) not something material (b) not to be thought of as belonging to a class of which there could be more than one member and (c) not something dependent for its existence on something distinct from itself ... as Aquinas himself says, the claim that God is the source of the universe implies that 'God is to be thought of as existing outside of the realm of existents as a cause from which pours forth everything that exists in all its variant forms.[24]

Having clarified what we mean by FMD and Classical Theism, we now move to argue for our thesis.

Can a Buddhist Be a Classical Theist?

Notice that when philosophers explain the interdependence and impermanence theses, they typically restrict their application. For example, Westerhoff applies the interdependence thesis to objects, Burton restricts the thesis to entities, and Garfield[25] restricts it to phenomena.[26] Now, for the purposes of the following discussion, we take it that objects, entities, phenomena, and things can all be used interchangeably. It follows that Garfield, Westerhoff, and Burton all restrict the theses in the same way. Nonetheless, since it's obvious that the application of the theses has a limit, the theses apply to what we will from here on refer to as "things."

Since the interdependence thesis and the impermanence thesis apply to things, much rides on what one means by "things." It would be beneficial to now clarify what we mean by a thing. It may be that the concept of a thing is too abstract to render in propositional form, nonetheless, the following statement of equivalence clarifies what is meant by the term and will elucidate the claim that God is not a thing:

Thing: T is a Thing iff T can possess a property.

On this definition, the God of Classical Theism can't be categorized as a "thing," as He is metaphysically simple and therefore cannot possess any properties.[27] He isn't a thing or being; He is ultimate reality. Therefore, one could affirm Classical Theism and still endorse the thesis that ultimately all things are without *svabhāva*.

Theism raises a problem for the Mere Buddhist only if God is construed as a thing among other things. If God possess *any* property then God would no longer be God, for then God's existence would depend on something else, namely, whatever properties God purportedly has or possesses. Moreover, if we suppose that God can gain or lose nonessential properties, then, given the doctrine of impermanence, God wouldn't retain His identity with each property He gains or losses and it follows that God would cease to exist from moment to moment. The Classical Theist needn't worry about any of these problems.

In what way, then, could we say that humans exist? Classical Theists typically are pluralists about modes of existence. Humans are said to exist but to some lesser degree. So they can say that humans exist but not in the same way that God exists. Like the Buddhist, the Classical Theist could assert that things that exist in this lesser sense are ultimately grounded in a mind. Not all Buddhist philosophers agree on just how to understand what it is for things to be grounded in a mind. For instance, the Yogācāra School maintains that nothing extramental exists, and thus that purportedly material beings are just disguised mental phenomena, and affirms that emptiness refers to the original, nondualistic state of mind that recognizes that no ontological distinction exists between the mind that knows and that which is known by the mind.[28] But, unlike the Yogācāra, Classical Theists who take this sort of route maintain that things are grounded in one specific mind, the Divine Mind. Classical Theists have held that, counterfactually, if God stopped thinking about a thing, that thing would cease to exist.[29] Following David Vander Laan, we call this the conservation thesis: The continued existence of created things depends on God's activity.[30] Clearly, if the conservation thesis is true, then it follows that things lack *svabhāva*. Classical Theists understand this point well. Speaking of Catherine of Sienna and Jonathan Edwards, Davies states the following:

> God is ultimate reality. And Catherine of Sienna, whose thinking is governed by the notion of God as source of everything, repeatedly says that only God is and she herself is not. In similar vein, Edwards explains that creatures are, in a sense, 'empty.' By creature being thus wholly and universally dependent on God', writes Edwards, 'it appears that the creature is nothing, and that God is all.'[31]

Their language is unexpectantly similar to Buddhist philosophers. Humans lack *svabhāva*. There is a sense in which God, *qua* ultimate reality, fully is and in that sense, humans, being mere things, are not.

Given that impermanence applies to things and humans are things, would it then follow that each human person exists only momentarily? If so, wouldn't this be problematic for those theists who want to hold on to personal identity? We suggest that Jonathan Edwards, a proponent of the impermanence thesis, can provide us with a solution to the problem.

For Edwards, God is constantly creating all things. Edwards states that, "God's upholding created substances, or causing its existence in each successive moment, is altogether equivalent to an immediate production out of nothing, at each moment ... So that this effect differs not at all from the first creation, but only circumstantially."[32] Things do not intrinsically have identity; as Edwards states, "there is no such thing as any identity or oneness in created objects, existing at different times ...."[33] Creature C^1 exists at T^1 but no longer exists at T^2. Instead, C^2, a nearly identical replica of C^1, exists at T^2. And, at T^3, C^2 goes out of existence, and God creates a nearly identical creature, C^3. While, each creature only exists momentarily, Edwards thought that creatures have identity over time in a sense. Edwards thought that individual instantaneous items, or slices, could collectively be joined together to constitute a transtemporal identity. Identity in this sense does not depend on a thing possessing intrinsic identity over time, but rather on "God's sovereign constitution."[34] In short, on Edwards's proposal of things, we may say that, creatures, including humans, lack intrinsic identity conditions over time and are extrinsically "held together" transtemporally by means of the operation of God's mind.

But is the existence of things that have transtemporal identities consistent with the impermanence thesis? If a transtemporal identity is a thing, then wouldn't it also cease to exist over time? It's not at all evident to us that typical philosophers writing in the Buddhist tradition, such as Westerhoff, have in mind something like Edwards's view when formulating the impermanence thesis. And if they do not, perhaps we may conclude that Edwards's view is not at odds with the impermanence thesis. Moreover, it isn't at all obvious that a given transtemporal identity should be considered a thing. Analytic philosophers, at least since the time of Gilbert Ryle, typically accept the view that when we observe a parade of a division of soldiers, we don't observe the soldiers *and* the division, for a division isn't something that exists over and above or independently of the individual soldiers marching thus and so.[35] Perhaps, when God creates a given transtemporal identity, it enters into a special relationship with God; perhaps, being extrinsically "held together" transtemporally by means of the operation of God's mind, its mode of existence is somewhere between Being itself and that of a conventional thing that is empty of own being.

Of course, one could always avoid talk of transtemporal identity and still account for personal identity, at least in some weak sense. For example, one might once again pull from the Yogācāra tradition, specifically utilizing its doctrine of storehouse consciousness, to help formulate a response to this concern. In order to make sense of how subjects can accumulate negative *karma* while at the same time affirming the impermanence thesis, Buddhists in the Yogācāra tradition argue that with each new experience that comes into existence, there is a seed of the immediately prior experience that exists within the current experience.[36] Mark Siderits describes the view in the following way:

> Now the hypothesis of karmic seeds was meant to explain how something in the remote past could be the cause of a present effect when everything is momentary. The idea was that the cause produced a seed, which produced another seed, etc. in an unbroken series, until conditions bring about the ripening of a seed to produce an impression.[37]

Inspired by this doctrine, one could say that there is a sense in which with each new slice of a transtemporal identity there exists a seed of the previous slice. In this way, it makes sense that some particular human slice is judged for the actions of a prior slice. There would be some metaphysical link between the two slices such the link could in a loose sense constitute an identity.

Masao Abe and Absolute Nonbeing

One might agree that with what we have argued so far, given the assumption that we have articulated FMD properly. But then one might reject our explication of FMD. For instance, one could argue that impermanence and interdependence don't just apply to things, but rather to Being itself. It is worthwhile to develop this line of objection in detail.

Our central claim is this: the theses discussed apply to things, and since God is not a thing, the theses do not apply to God. But there are Buddhists who would object to this line of reasoning. Masao Abe, for instance, would argue that our explication of Buddhist metaphysics is inadequate because it doesn't go far enough.

Abe maintains that when Buddhists say that all things are impermanent and that, without exception, everything is dependent on something else, they mean to deny the Brahmanical notion that there is an Absolute and unconditioned reality on which the existence of all things depends. Briefly, the Brahmanical tradition affirms that, despite appearances, all that exists is the unitary being of Brahman. There exists one transcendent substance, Brahman, and all so-called "things" are really just modes or aspects of Brahman. Buddhists and Brahmans both deny the reality of the world of appearances. But Buddhists reject Brahmanism; they categorically deny the existence of Brahman and replace the notion of a transcendent reality with the notion of dependent origination (*pratītya-samutpāda*).

Putting the point in Platonic terms, Abe maintains that Buddhists reject both transcendence and immanence. He writes:

> Like Plato, Mahāyana Buddhism insists that everything in this world is mutable, transient, and subject to time and change. Unlike Plato, however, Mahāyana Buddhism does not expound the existence of an immutable, eternal, and transcendent realm beyond this world. There is *nothing* eternal, transcendent, and real behind or beyond this transitory world.[38]

And,

> [T]here can be nothing whatever ... that is more real and eternal, and that lies behind the interdependence of everything. This is true whether one speaks of the temporal or non-temporal realms, sensual or suprasensual realms. In Buddhism, one cannot emphasize too strongly the interdependence of everything.[39]

Emphasizing that "nothingness" (*śūnyatā*) is not to be understood in contrast to "somethingness," Abe writes, "The Buddhist idea of dependent origination therefore implies that there can be absolutely nothing whatsoever that is real and eternal—behind this actual world."[40] Put another way, again in Platonic terms, *śūnyatā* is not merely the denial of the world of becoming, the realm of appearances, together with the denial of Being; rather, it is Absolute Nonbeing, the double negation of both becoming and Being. Elsewhere, explicating Abe's view, Baldwin writes:

> Abe cautions Western readers not to associate the emptiness of *sunyata* with Parmenidean non-being. According to the metaphysics of *sunyata*, there is no ontological priority of relative being over non-being; *sunyata* is prior to any distinction between relative being and non-being ... According to Abe, both being and non-being are conditioned; neither has logical priority over the other and both depend on something else, the non-conditioned, i.e., *sunyata*. Abe writes, "Sunyata is realized not only by negating the 'eternalist' view [the Platonic and Parmenidean view of being] but also by negating the 'nihilistic' view [the negation of being, i.e., Parmenidean non-being]." Because it negates both being and non-being, the emptiness of *sunyata* is absolute non-being ... Absolute nothingness.[41]

To sum up, according to Abe, Nāgārjuna took up the Mahayana standpoint of emptiness, within which one is liberated from every illusory point of view connected with either affirmation or negation, being or nonbeing, and called that standpoint the *Middle Way*.[42] In turn, Abe calls Nāgārjuna's *Middle Way* the standpoint of absolute nothingness, a standpoint that amounts to the rejection of both Being ("Eternalism") and Nonbeing ("Annihilationism"), dichotomy prevalent in Western Philosophy. Both Being and Nonbeing are "mutually inseparable and relative concepts" and as such are conceptual abstractions. According to Abe, the Buddha taught that all things are dependent on all other things (*pratitya-samutpada*) and that all reality is empty of intrinsic nature (*svabhāva-śūnya*). The God of Classical Theism is not empty of intrinsic nature; God's essence is to exist. Moreover, God, the most real reality, transcends the created order of things. However, as Abe argues, there is no room for any transcendent reality on Buddhism. Therefore, the *Madhyamaka* standpoint is inconsistent with Classical Theism.

In response, first, it is important to note that the thesis of this chapter is that "Classical Theism is compatible with FMD, at least, insofar as FMD is understood by Garfield." In a sense, because Abe's construal of emptiness is quite different than Garfield's, Abe's construal of Buddhist metaphysics is irrelevant to the focus of our thesis, which is limited to FMD *as understood by Garfield*. Thus, given Garfield's view, our arguments for the impermanence and interdependent theses could still be considered sound. One would simply restrict the applications of the theses to all "things," and, therefore wouldn't apply them to God.

Let's take a subject named John as an example to help better clarify our point. John grew up in a Buddhist household. While John becomes convinced that all "things" are impermanent and interdependent, he becomes less inclined to think that these theses apply to Being simpliciter. That is, suppose that John becomes much more open to the possibility that existence is not exhausted by the existence of things, but there is, in some sense, a sort of existence beyond or above that of which he is aware by means of his senses. In such a state, John goes to his local Buddhist temple and asks a particular Buddha to give him some of the Buddha's merited grace to aid him in his own journey toward enlightenment. He remains emphatic that the world isn't how it appears. He agrees that the "things" that he is naturally attached to are "empty" and he should become detached from them in order to ease suffering. This causes John to hang a poster displaying the Eight-Fold Path (this will be discussed in more detail in Chapter Four) so that he would be reminded of how he should act. And John continues to read Buddhist philosophers, such as Garfield, and primary texts of Buddhism, including, say, Buddha's Discourses (the *Digha Nikaya, Majjhima Nikaya, Samyutta Nikaya, Khuddaka Nikaya,* and the *Anguttara Nikaya*) and Yogācāra texts, such as the *Yogācārabhūmi-śāstra* and the *Saṃdhinirmocana-sūtra*, to help him have the right understanding of Ultimate Reality. Are we really to say that John is not a Buddhist just because he doesn't explicitly deny the possibility of transcendent realities and doesn't explicitly endorse Abe's metaphysical interpretation of *Madhyamaka*?

All Buddhists need to correct their inclinations with right understanding. Along these lines, Abe (and Buddhists who agree with his interpretation of emptiness) would say the John lacks a right understanding of emptiness. From that standpoint, realizing *nirvana* involves realizing Absolute Nonbeing, which in turn involves rejecting the Being/Nonbeing dichotomy. Again, according to Abe, any analysis of emptiness that allows for the existence of any sort of transcendent reality is fundamentally flawed. However, even given Abe's position, we needn't say that John's not a Buddhist. One could say that John has attachments to false conceptions that prevent him from (fully) realizing enlightenment. John would be a seriously misinformed Buddhist who accepts a flawed understanding of emptiness. His inclinations to believe otherwise are among the things he needs to rid himself of so as to have right understanding. This is roughly analogous to how a Christian layperson might implicitly affirm all manner of heretical views about the doctrines of the Trinity and the Incarnation but still be considered a Christian. Many laypeople, especially those new to the faith, don't know any better, and so affirm doctrinal errors without culpability. However, once having been shown why this or that view has been deemed to be heretical, it is incumbent on a Christian to give that view up. It is spiritually dangerous for a Christian to persist in holding a heretical belief. Similarly, Abe could say that while John is on the path to enlightenment, he won't likely achieve it or will not achieve a full measure of enlightenment if he persists in accepting a false conception of emptiness.

It is important whether Abe's conception or Garfield's conception of emptiness is correct. If Abe has the correct standpoint, then Garfield's standpoint is incorrect, and vice versa. If there are all things considered good reasons to side with Abe, that would make the success of our arguments much less interesting. But even if Abe is correct, it would not follow that our project is a failure, for we still will have shown that Garfield's explication of emptiness is consistent with Classical Theism. While Abe's view has much to be said in favor of it, we don't think that it is necessary for a Buddhist to take it up. Abe's understanding of emptiness is metaphysically robust, and its articulation involves some heavy-duty metaphysical speculation. On the other hand, Garfield's thesis is both modest and non-negotiable; it follows fairly straightforwardly from the Four Noble Truths. While it is not our place to answer definitively whether Garfield's or Abe's interpretation of emptiness is correct, we take it that for those within the Buddhist tradition, there are good reasons for preferring Garfield's more metaphysically modest view.

In *The Shorter Exhortation to Mālunkya Cūḷa Mālunkyovāda Sutta*, we read about a frustrated disciple of the Buddha who was wrestling with several metaphysical quandaries. Among other things, he was perplexed about whether or not the cosmos was eternal, whether the cosmos is finite or infinite, and whether or not the soul and the body are the same. The disciple was so upset that he threatened to renounce his training and go back to his prior life. Buddha pointed out that he never claimed to provide answers to such questions. He never claimed to disclose answers to any of these pairs of positions. He took no stance on such things because asking and answering such questions are distracting and unnecessary. Responding to his disciple, the Buddha says that he did not disclose answers to the questions because doing so is "not connected with the goal," it is "not fundamental to the holy life," and it does not "lead to disenchantment, dispassion,

cessation, calming, direct knowledge, self-awakening, unbinding."[43]
He continues:

> And what is disclosed by me? 'This is stress,' is disclosed by me.
> 'This is the origination of stress,' is disclosed by me. 'This is the
> cessation of stress,' is disclosed by me. 'This is the path of practice
> leading to the cessation of stress,' is disclosed by me. And why are
> they disclosed by me? Because they are connected with the goal,
> are fundamental to the holy life. They lead to disenchantment,
> dispassion, cessation, calming, direct knowledge, self-awakening,
> unbinding. That's why they are disclosed by me.[44]

In another sermon, Vacchagotta asked Buddha "Is there a self?"
and Buddha remained silent. Vacchagotta then asked "Is there not a
self?" but again Buddha remained silent. After Vacchagotta departed,
Ānanda, Buddha's closest disciple, asked why he remained silent.
The Buddha replied that if he told Vacchagotta that there is a self
then he would be committing himself to the Brahmanical view,
and that if he said there was not self then he would be siding with
the Annihilationist's view. The Buddha remained silent because
he thought that there were no adequate responses to the sorts of
questions Vacchagotta asked.[45]

Following this line of thinking, we can address Abe's objection in
a similar way. Garfield and Abe provide different and incompatible
interpretations of emptiness, but must a Buddhist take a stance on
which of these is correct? Going farther, must a Buddhist accept *any*
particular metaphysical teaching that goes beyond the Four Noble
Truths? Individual Buddhists may have reasons for taking various
stances about this or that point. On the other hand, individual
Buddhists may see no reason to take up any of them. At any rate, we
think that we've given a convincing enough case in favor of working
with Garfield's metaphysically modest analysis of emptiness. We take
it that it would be possible for a Buddhist who accepts Garfield's

interpretation of emptiness to go on and accept Classical Theism without contradiction or incoherence.

Creation *ex nihilo*

Perhaps one could argue that FMD is not compatible with Classical Theism, not because FMD entails a rejection of God, but rather because the interdependence thesis is at odds with the doctrine of creation *ex nihilo*, the view that God created the universe out of nothing.[46] The interdependence thesis as defined might be interpreted in such a way as to entail that there could be no beginning to our universe. Rather, each state of affairs relates to another state of affairs. There can be no first state of affairs as that state of affairs would need to be connected to another. Put in another way, if X is interconnected with Y and Z, then X's explanation for its existence is grounded (at least in part) in Y and Z. X can't exist without Y and Z. There are five points that we will make in response.

First, it's not clear to us that Classical Theism entails the doctrine of creation *ex nihilo*. While the doctrine is an infallible dogma in both the Catholic and Orthodox traditions, we don't see why someone couldn't affirm Classical Theism and at the same time affirm that the universe has always existed with God. The universe could of course still be grounded in God's Mind, but one might contend that God's Mind has thought about the universe in such a way that, for all eternity, it has always existed (or at least, some universe that resembles past universes).

Second, if all one means by causal dependence is that "All events in time … occur in dependence to prior causes and conditions, and all states of affairs cease when the cause and conditions that are necessary for their occurrence cease," then one could still in some sense affirm God as a cause of a particular state of affairs (e.g., the creation of the universe). Since God is outside of time, and since God is not a thing, God needn't and indeed *can't* have a prior cause.

Third, perhaps one might have an even more robust understanding of interdependence and find our second point weak. Nonetheless, there still seems to be a strong response to be made here. It seems perfectly sensible for God to exist without there being states of affairs (at least, as it pertains to phenomena) and for there to be such a thing as T^1 where God initiated a set of interconnected states. God could have created a set or sets of interconnected states simultaneously. In this case, while it is true that X, Y, and Z are interdependent such that each can't be explained without the other, nonetheless, God would still ground the ultimate explanation of why this set began to exist in the first place. One could, then, have a very robust sense of interdependence and still affirm creation *ex nihilo*.

Fourth, it might be such that, since our language about God is analogical, we can't (fully) understand what it means for God to create anything. Perhaps, God's creating something out of nothing does violate the principle of interdependence if we understand "God created" in a strict univocal sense. However, if our language about God doesn't map onto God in a strict univocal sense, then it could be that whatever "God created" means is compatible with the interdependence thesis.

Finally, it seems that the Classical Theist, if anything, has an advantage over other types of theists when making sense of how there could be a creation at all. One cannot explain why the realm of things exists by appealing to one of the things in the realm. Herbert McCabe puts it best:

> It is clear that we reach out to, but do not reach an answer to our ultimate question, how come anything instead of nothing? But we are able to exclude some answers. If God is whatever answers our question, how come everything? Then evidently he is not to be included amongst everything. God cannot be a thing, an existent

among others. It is not possible that God and the universe should add up to make two. Again, if we are to speak of God as causing the existence of everything, it is clear that we must not mean that he makes the universe out of anything.[47]

While we don't think the objection dealt with here is successful against our main thesis, we do recognize that there are various other objections which challenge the coherence of the specific conception of God that we have advocated. We now move on to engage objections found within the Buddhist tradition that are directed against Classical Theism. These criticisms do not stem from what we call Mere Buddhism but rather have much in common with contemporary criticisms developed by analytic atheists in the field of philosophy of religion.

Buddhist Objections to Classical Theism

There is a long-standing tradition within the Buddhist literature that there is no ultimate, unchanging Deity. Even as early as the *Dīgha Nikāya* (*c.* second or third century CE), we see the gods portrayed poorly as the protagonist of the text looks for a deity who is omniscient but none can be found.[1] There is, of course, the objection that we resolved in Chapter One, namely, that the existence of God is incompatible with the impermanence thesis. Roger Jackson develops this argument in another way that is worth mentioning here. He argues that a Supreme unchanging God is incompatible with impermanence because there are no coherent or workable models of unchanging persons interacting with changing persons:

> It really is Buddhism's emphasis on universal impermanence that is at the root of its aversion to the concept of God. For example, Dharmakirti argues that only momentary entities can exist because to exist means to be causally efficacious; a permanent, unchanging being cannot be causally efficacious because its immutability entails that it cannot interact with other entities; therefore it does not exist.[2]

There are various other reasons as to why theism is rejected in the traditional Buddhist literature. Objections range from the traditional problem of evil to objections relating to the metaphysics of causality. In this chapter, we will respond to three objections in turn, starting with Jackson's argument from impermanence. We will argue that each objection fails to consider the God of Classical Theism. Instead, the objections often assume a God who can be understood univocally. These objections assume one of the various forms of personalism found within the Hindu tradition.[3] Answering these objections will lead us to the next chapter, in which we argue that not only do traditional Buddhist objections to Classical Theism fail, but also the contemporary arguments from the analytic tradition do as well.

Objection I: Argument from Interaction

Steinkellner summarizes the interaction objection to Classical Theism as follows:

> They therefore argue against the possibility of any interaction between a permanent factor and impermanent entities: not only is it impossible, but also because it is unnecessary, meaningless. Moreover, Hindu concepts of a permanent creating factor are modelled on an analogy to human activity: change in everything thus also presupposes a planning consciousness. Theologically speaking, it may be then worth considering the question of whether the focus on continuity and the human analogy of causal activity— both referring to the finite realm—are necessary to a discourse on God.[4]

One Buddhist text puts the problem like this: "Whatever is existent is exclusively momentary, since, if it were non-momentary, it would be excluded from being a real entity because of its contradiction to causal efficacy (*arthakiya*), (for a real entity) is characterized by having this (causal efficacy)."[5]

One can look at Elenore Stump's work to see how this objection can have a more contemporary glossing. In *God of the Bible and God of the Philosophers*, Stump discusses how those who are opposed to Classical Theism will argue that an immutable God can't answer prayers,[6] personally engage His creation,[7] or have a will that is in any way dependent on His creation.[8] She summarizes her objection as follows:

And now the problem is evident. How could *being* say 'you' to anything? And who could use second-personal address in any locution towards God if God is being alone? And, in general, in the biblical stories, there is a readily discernible image of God in human beings, and conversely a readily discernible divine original in God for the image of God in human beings. By contrast, there seems to be so little in common between God and human beings on the characterization of the God of classical theism as I have described it here that it is hard to imagine why anyone would suppose that human beings are made in the image of such a God.[9]

Stump, however, rejects the idea that it's impossible for God to be eternally present to and genuinely communicate with His creation. Stump gives the following scenario to help develop her response:

> So consider Erwin Abbott's famous *Flatland*, a story about a two-dimensional world occupied by sentient two-dimensional creatures. In *Flatland*, one of these two-dimensional creatures, a sentient square, comes into conversation with a sentient sphere, who is an inhabitant of a three-dimensional world. The sphere has a terrible time explaining his three-dimensional world to his new friend, the two-dimensional square. As Flatland presents things, there is more than one mode of spatial existence for sentient beings. There is both the Flatland two-dimensional mode of spatial existence and the three-dimensional mode of spatial existence … If Flatland were finite and linearly ordered with an absolute middle, there might be an absolute Flatland here, which in the Flatland world could be occupied by only one Flatlander at a time. Nonetheless, if Flatland were small enough, then from the point of view of a human observer in the three-dimensional world, all of Flatland could be here at once. And yet it would not follow and it would not be true that all of Flatland would be here with respect to any occupant of Flatland. So it could be the case both that only one thing in Flatland could be here at once (with respect to the occupants of Flatland) and also that all of Flatland could be here at once (with respect to the inhabitants of the three-dimensional world).

The reason for this apparently paradoxical claim is that all of Flatland can be encompassed within the metaphysically bigger here of the three-dimensional world.[10]

Since God lacks any potentiality, there is no succession in His being. His being is fully present all at once.[11] God nonetheless can still communicate with His creation. Stump likens God to the three-dimensional world: just as a three-dimensional being could experience the two-dimensional world all at once, God can see all things that will ever exist at once. Moreover, it could be such that God, as is the case for the three-dimensional being in our scenario, has eternally acted upon the two-dimensional world in such a way that God's one eternal act encompasses His initial communication with His creation, His willing his creation to respond to His communication, and His response to His creation. According to those living in a two-dimensional world, this decree might come across as distinct and separate acts. But, of course, a being who is immutable couldn't have multiple distinct actions.

All this could be hard for two-dimensional creatures to understand; it may be exceedingly difficult for creatures like them to understand how a three-dimensional being can really relate to their two-dimensional world. Nonetheless, the three-dimensional being's communication with the two-dimensional world would be genuine. God's one act, while it appears to us in this dimension as multiple acts, encompasses His willing us to act and His response to this willing. God can thus be immutable and genuinely communicate with His creatures. It is, then, not impossible for an immutable being to genuinely interact with mutable beings.

Perhaps the objector thinks the sort of view described here leads to determinism or even worse, fatalism. And one might think that determinism is incompatible with genuine engagement with the world. We will pick up more on this objection in the next chapter.

For now, we move to engage another standard objection found in the Buddhist literature.

Objection II: Causes Must Resemble Their Effect

As Burton points out,[12] in the Buddhist literature, there is a standard objection relating to causality that goes something like this:

1. All effects that come from God must resemble God.
2. The world is constantly changing and thus doesn't resemble God.
Therefore,
3. The world isn't an effect brought about from God.

Behind (1) is an assumption that effects must resemble their cause. Call this assumption the resemblance assumption, or RA. Is RA plausible? RA seems to us to be extremely ambiguous. To what extent must an effect resemble its cause? Tyler is typing on the keyboard currently, does the typing need to resemble him? We suppose that it resembles Tyler's mind insofar as what he types is what he wants to convey. Or, take the example of Erik lifting a water bottle up and drinking its contents. How does drinking water resemble Erik? We suppose that in some sense Erik is made up of water, but is there something more to resembling Erik than this? Finally, take the example of picking up a controller and playing a video game. There is in some sense a way in which the video game's character resembles the player's intelligence and desire to win. So, perhaps there is a very loose sense in which the effect must resemble its cause. But, if we define RA very loosely, the impermanent world could nevertheless somewhat resemble God. For example, according to Aquinas's Fiftth Way, the world and the things contained within it, get their *telos* from God's mind and thus reflect in some way God's mind. The world doesn't need to resemble God completely. Of course, if we define RA to entail complete resemblance, then it's likely to seem *prima facie* implausible.

We are not aware of a good reason as to why we should construe RA to entail exactness or close resemblance. In fact, we are not sure what is to be gained by explicitly endorsing RA to begin with. Perhaps behind the endorsement of RA is the idea that the effect can't have more reality than the cause. Construed thus, RA is recognizably related to a scholastic principle that contemporary philosophers might know as the Precontainment Principle endorsed by Rene Descartes, i.e., that "there can be nothing in an effect which was not previously present in the cause."[13] Of course, there is nothing incompatible with suggesting that both the scholastic causal principle is plausible and that God created the universe. The universe wouldn't have more reality than God. God just *is* Ultimate Reality. In fact, Descartes takes this principle and develops a type of ontological argument for God's existence in *Meditations on First Philosophy*, Meditation Five. We think the Buddhist opponent to theism must develop RA more rigorously in order for the objection to be compelling. The historical Buddhist literature on God's existence, unfortunately, typically isn't sufficiently technical to allow for this. Philosophers drawing on this literature have their work cut out for them.

Objection III: The Problem of Evil

While the Buddhist literature isn't full of technical arguments on the subject, especially arguments that would be recognized by contemporary analytic philosophers, there is discussion of the problem of evil. Steinkellner puts it as follows:

> Real arguments are still rare in the literature. Rejection on the grounds of theodicy, however, already occurs on various occasions. If God created the universe and conducted its order, man would

not be morally responsible and God would not be benevolent, since evils and suffering are his creation too.[14]

Philosophers have come to recognize that there are at least two versions of the problem of evil. First, there is the logical problem of evil, which advocates that there is a logical inconsistency with the existence of God and evil. Not many find this argument to be compelling in the contemporary literature. This is in part, due to Alvin Plantinga's Free Will Defense.[15] Instead, as it relates to the problem of evil, what is primarily discussed is the evidential problem of evil. The proponent of the evidential problem argues that the appearance of gratuitous evil makes the existence of God improbable. We can put it in the following schematic form:

1. For some actual evils E we know of, we cannot think of any morally justifying reason for permitting them.
2. Therefore, probably, there are not any morally justifying reasons for permitting them.
3. If God exists, he would not permit E if there were no morally justifying reason for permitting them.
4. Therefore, probably, God does not exist.[16]

For sake of charity, let's assume that the Buddhist objector has something like this in mind. How could a theist respond to this argument? We think the best response is to deny (2). Just because one cannot think of a morally justifying reason for God allowing some instance of evil E, it doesn't follow that there isn't a morally justifying reason. Specifically, we endorse the thesis of skeptical theism. We don't believe that any creature is in the position to know what God would or wouldn't do when it comes to most instances of evil.[17]

Oftentimes, the skeptical theist will utilize analogies to help motivate her thesis. We will continue with this tradition by giving the following example:

> Eli is two years old. Given Eli's cognitive limitations, Eli thinks that it's a good idea to jump off a swing as it's moving back and forth. However, upon jumping off, Eli's arm gets caught on a nail. Eli is now hanging by the skin of his arm. Eli quickly goes to the hospital where they begin putting shots on Eli's wound as his father holds him down. Confused as to why his dad would pin him down and allow strangers to hurt him, Eli cries out to his father in desperation. Eli can't think of any reason as to why his father would do this.[18]

There are clearly sufficiently good reasons for Eli's father to hold Eli down and to allow doctors to poke him with needles. However, it's beyond Eli's ken to understand why. Eli isn't in the epistemic position to make a judgment.

Similarly, there is an epistemic gap between mature adults and God. As mentioned in the previous chapter, God isn't merely another being. Rather, God is Being itself. We cannot grasp God's intrinsic predicates in a univocal way. We have to understand God by way of analogy. It seems that, if anything, there is a bigger epistemic gap between mature human adults and God than there is between young children and mature human adults. We simply are not in the position to jump from (1) to (2). Maybe if God was merely a superman like human, we could track more with God's understanding. However, as Isaiah, a Prophet from the Hebrew Bible, says, "For my thoughts are not your thoughts, neither are your ways my ways," declares the LORD. "As the heavens are higher than the earth, so are my ways higher than your ways and my thoughts than your thoughts."[19] Or as Paul in the New Testament puts it, "For the foolishness of God is wiser than human wisdom, and the weakness of God is stronger than human strength."[20] This recognition exists also in the Islamic tradition. Surah 2:30 states, "And [mention, O Muhammad], when your Lord said to the angels, 'Indeed, I will make upon the earth a successive authority.' They said, 'Will You place upon it one who causes corruption therein and sheds blood, while we declare Your praise and sanctify You?'

Allah said, 'Indeed, I know that which you do not know.'"[21] And even more explicit, in Surah 2:216, the Qur'an states, " … But perhaps you hate a thing and it is good for you; and perhaps you love a thing and it is bad for you. And Allah Knows, while you know not."[22]

The assumption that we should be able to formulate theodicies and explain why God would allow some instance of evil seems aimed at a univocally personalistic conception of God. Again, this would make sense given that the Buddhist critiques are commonly aimed at various personalistic conceptions of theism. These sorts of critiques, however, lack force when it comes to Classical Theism.

Skeptical Theism Refuted?

There has been a recent trend, however, in the contemporary literature that argues that if the thesis of skeptical theism is true, then we have a defeater for trusting God. God, for example, could deceive or permit deception as it pertains to His revelation. Maybe we cannot come up with sufficiently good reasons as to why God would deceive us about who He is or what He has done, but that needn't worry the skeptical theist. She is already committed to the view that it is beyond a creature's cognitive ability to grasp why God would permit some instance of evil. The problem is that the skeptical theist isn't skeptical enough, or so the argument goes. If one embraces skepticism as it pertains to the problem of evil, then one should embrace skepticism as it pertains to divine revelation, too. This argument has recently been forcefully presented by Hud Hudson and Erik Wielenberg.

Summing up his argument, Hudson writes:

> If there is a morally obligating reason for God to deceive me, then I am deceived. If there is no morally justifying reason for God to deceive me, then I am not deceived. If there is a morally justifying reason for God to deceive me, then either I am or am not deceived

depending on God's other purposes. Skeptical theists would remind me that I am utterly in the dark about which of those three antecedents is satisfied. And thus the darkness expands so that I am also utterly in the dark about whether I am deceived in the most comprehensive, irresistible, and undetectable fashion.[23]

Similarly, Erik Wielenberg's argument[24] can be summarized as follows:

> 1. If skeptical theism is true, then, for any divine assertion that p, we lack justification for believing that it is false or unlikely that God's act of intentionally asserting that p when p is false has beyond-our-ken justification.
> 2. If, for any divine assertion that p, we lack justification for believing that it is false or unlikely that God's act of intentionally asserting that p when p is false has beyond-our-ken justification, then we do not know p if p has word-of-God justification (unless we have good reason for thinking that, even if God has some justification for lying about p, God does not act on that justification).
> 3. So, skeptical theism implies that we do not know any proposition that has word-of-God justification only (unless we have good reason for thinking that, even if God has some justification for lying, God does not act on that justification).
> 4. We do not have good reason for thinking that, even if God has some justification for lying, God does not act on that justification.
> 5. Therefore, skeptical theism implies that we do not know any proposition that has word-of-God justification only.[25]

Are Wielenberg and Hudson right? We think not. Specifically, regarding Wielenberg's construal, the skeptical theist could simply flat out deny (1).

> 1. If skeptical theism is true, then, for any divine assertion that p, we lack justification for believing that it is false or unlikely that God's act of intentionally asserting that p when p is false has beyond-our-ken justification.

Why should the skeptical theist think that if skeptical theism is true then we lack justification for believing that God has not deceived us? Elsewhere, we argue that a proper functionalist will be unfazed by this argument. Proper functionalism is a theory of warrant (the property of a belief that turns a true belief into knowledge) that goes as follows:

S's belief that P is warranted, iff ...

1. The belief in question is formed by way of cognitive faculties that are properly functioning.

2. The cognitive faculties in question are aimed at the production of true beliefs.

3. The design plan is a good one. That is, when a belief is formed by way of truth-aimed cognitive proper function in the sort of environment for which the cognitive faculties in question were designed, there is a high objective probability that the resulting belief is true.

4. The belief is formed in the sort of environment for which the cognitive faculties in question were designed.[26]

This theory of warrant is, in part, a response to the skeptical scenarios mentioned above. As many have noted, the historical arguments for the existence of other minds aren't too impressive.[27] Nonetheless, belief in other minds can still be warranted. If, for example, subject S was designed to produce the belief in other minds, S's design plan is successfully aimed at truth, her faculties are functioning properly, and S is in the environment for which she was designed, then S's belief that there are other minds would be warranted. S's wouldn't need access to whether her belief likely is warranted; the belief merely needs to be the product of the proper functionalist constraints. In a similar way, it might be such that S is designed to produce the belief in both of the following:

A. God is not deceiving subject S about divine revelation.

B. Subject S is not in the position to judge whether God would likely permit an instance of evil.

It's not problematic to affirm that S was designed to produce both A and B. Moreover, it definitely doesn't entail that if S accepts B then she cannot be warranted with respect to believing A. Wielenberg and Hudson need to do more work to show that this is the case. We summarize our response here elsewhere as follows:

> On the other hand, given proper functionalism, perhaps a theist can insist that if one has reflected on this general problem of divine deception and still has the strong seeming that God's revelation is truthful and reliable, her beliefs formed by way of divine testimony can still be warranted—assuming such beliefs were formed by way of the proper functionalist constraints.[28]

As Perry Hendricks has noted, this response isn't only available to proper functionalists.[29] If one endorses phenomenal conservatism, one could make a similar move. Phenomenal Conservatism is the thesis that S's belief that p is justified if it seems to S that p and S is without a defeater for p. Going back to the case of belief in other minds, S could recognize that there are no good arguments for belief in other minds. Nonetheless, S could have a seeming that other minds exist. And, assuming S is without a defeater for her belief that other minds exist, S possesses some justification for her belief. Coming back to the present objection, it could be that S has a seeming for both (A) and (B) and she may well be without a defeater for what she's inclined to believe. If so, there is no reason to think that the acceptance of (B) entails a rejection of (A). In specifically responding to Wielenberg, Hendricks makes this point clearer:

> Consider the consequent of Premise (5), which states: we lack justification for believing that it is false or unlikely that God's act of intentionally asserting that p when p is false has beyond-our-ken

justification. Call the proposition it is unlikely (or false) that God's act of intentionally asserting that p when p is false has beyond-our-ken justification 'E'. Suppose S is a skeptical theist, an adherent of phenomenal conservatism, that it seems to her that E is the case, and that she does not have a defeater for her seeming. If this is possible, then it is possible for the antecedent of (5) to be true and its consequent false, in which case Premise (5) is false—or, at least, the adherent of phenomenal conservatism will reject Premise (5). Therefore, the skeptical theist that adheres to phenomenal conservatism should reject Premise (5), and Wielenberg's argument along with it. Perhaps, however, Wielenberg would argue that S has a defeater for her seeming that E and hence does not have justification for believing it. It is unclear just how this argument would go ... For example, when one sees a stick bent in the water and it seems to her to be bent, she has a defeater for her seeming because she knows that her seeming is not reliable in that environment. But it does not ... leave the skeptical theist in a situation like this: she does not, in virtue of her skeptical theism, have reason to think that the processes responsible for forming her seeming in respect to E are in fact unreliable ....[30]

It seems to us that skeptical theism is a perfectly natural response to the problem of evil, especially in light of the Classical understanding of how God should be perceived. If the thesis is undefeated, it seems like this Buddhist objection, like the ones before it, fails, too. The Buddhist then can recognize a bad objection that is discussed within her tradition and move on from it. There is nothing within Mere Buddhism that entails that she accepts that the problem of evil is a good objection to theism, especially in light of the criticisms raised here. Having now engaged various objections found within the Buddhist literature, we now move to consider contemporary objections to Classical Theism.

3

Contemporary Objections to Classical Theism

Perhaps the reader is now unimpressed with the more traditionally styled objections to our project that may be espoused by Buddhists. While the reader might see that there is no necessary connection between these objections and the claims of Mere Buddhism, the reader might still be skeptical about the sort of theism that we have explicated and relied on throughout this project. Classical Theism has gone out of style in mainstream philosophy of religion.[1] If there are contemporary objections that would devastate Classical Theism, then the project of this book is bound to fail. In this chapter, we tackle various contemporary objections to Classical Theism. Our hope is that upon defending Classical Theism from contemporary objections, the reader will be more confident in the sort of theism defended in the volume. If we can motivate that Classical Theism is coherent, however, the reader should judge the merits of the project based on whether our synthesis works rather than objecting to theism that we espouse. In this chapter we will engage five objections aimed at undermining Classical Theism. We start with discussing the argument from temporal knowledge.

Objection I: Objection from Temporal Knowledge

Our first objection goes as follows:

> If God is strongly immutable, God cannot know tensed facts, specifically the current time. For example, I know that right now, it

is 4:33. I didn't know this until it was 4:33. In about 60 seconds, I'll no longer know that it is 4:33. Instead, I'll know that it is 4:34. My knowledge changes as time changes. But how can God know what time it is given that God is strongly immutable? God can't change in the same way that you and I change. So, God must not know all true propositions.[2]

Norman Kretzmann glosses this argument in the following syllogism:

1. A perfect being is not subject to change.
2. A perfect being knows everything.
3. A being that knows everything always knows what time it is.
4. A being that always knows what time it is is subject to change.

Therefore:

5. A perfect being is subject to change.

Therefore:

6. A perfect being is not a perfect being.

Finally, therefore,

7. There is no perfect being.[3]

Are omniscience and strong immutability really in conflict with each other? Must we abandon Classical Theism's central tenant, that God is strongly immutable? We think not. There are at least two reasons in favor of answering "no" to this question. First, this objection assumes presentism, a theory of time that says only the present is ontologically real. On a B-theory, specifically eternalism, the past and future are just as real as the present. If this is the case, then, ultimately, there is no "now" to know. While, it would seem as if it really is 4:57 pm right now, this would just be because of one's limited reference point. All of time exists, and, analogically speaking, God can see the past, present, and future all at the same time. But many Buddhists are presentists.

Thus, there is a need for additional responses that don't depend on this specific theory of time. We think that Thomas Sullivan provides us with resources for making this response.

In retelling Aquinas's view on how God knows, Thomas Sullivan states the following:

> Thomas reasons that since the power to form the statement of facts lies within the human mind, and since God knows whatever is in the power of his creatures, God knows all the statements of fact that can be formed. But since the divine mind, unlike the human mind, has no need to unify in a statement an understanding of reality taken in bit by bit (*unum redigere per modum compositionis vel divisionis, enuntiationem formando*), it does not understand stable facts by forming statements of them (*scit enuntiabilia non per modum enuntiabilium*) … In a more contemporary idiom, we may say that God's knowledge is nonpropositional, i.e., God does not form propositions to understand the world. And if God knows everything without forming propositions, then there is something wrong with the challenge to state in propositional form just what God represents to himself of temporal events. With his customary terseness, Thomas is thus proposing a remarkable solution to the Argument from Omniscience. God knows all that we know about temporal events, but in a way that we cannot adequately represent to ourselves.[4]

Roughly, the idea is that God possesses knowledge in a different way than His creatures do. Given His simplicity, God is identical to His knowledge. Thus, while it is right to say that God and creatures both possess knowledge, we need to understand that God possesses knowledge differently from what we mean when we say that humans possess knowledge.[5] Being creatures, we can only understand God's knowledge by analogy. It follows that God's knowledge cannot be subject to our own categories and limits. For instance, we possess knowledge about the current time; there will be changes in knowledge with respect to us. But because God knows truths in a different way than we do, it doesn't follow that there will necessarily be changes with respect to God's knowledge.

Perhaps one thinks that this isn't so much a response to the original objection, but an *ad hoc* way to avoid the objection altogether.[6] We'd like to assure our reader that this move isn't so at all. As shown in the last chapter, not being able to predict God's actions or how God operates is exactly what we would expect on Classical Theism. The response is well motivated and fits naturally within the overall Classical Theist hypothesis. And, once again, this is the view of God that has been accepted since the era of the great philosophical Greeks and perhaps even in the later Israelite theology.[7] Having responded to this objection, we now move to respond to the objection that the God of Classical Theism isn't omniscient as He lacks experiential knowledge.

Objection II: Objection from Experiential knowledge

With respect to the mind–body problem, physicalism is the thesis that the human mind is ultimately reducible to physical stuff, usually the brain. One famous counterexample to physicalism is the color-blind Mary case:

> Mary is a brilliant scientist who is, for whatever reason, forced to investigate the world from a black and white room via a black and white television monitor. She specializes in the neurophysiology of vision and acquires, let us suppose, all the physical information there is to obtain about what goes on when we see ripe tomatoes, or the sky, and use terms like 'red', 'blue', and so on. She discovers, for example, just which wavelength combinations from the sky stimulate the retina, and exactly how this produces *via* the central nervous system the contraction of the vocal chords and expulsion

of air from the lungs that results in the uttering of the sentence 'The sky is blue'. … What will happen when Mary is released from her black and white room or is given a color television monitor? Will she *learn* anything or not? It seems just obvious that she will learn something about the world and our visual experience of it. But then is it inescapable that her previous knowledge was incomplete. But she had *all* the physical information. *Ergo* there is more to have than that, and Physicalism is false.[8]

There is a kind of knowledge—call it experiential knowledge—that one can only gain by experiencing the world. In this case, there is something about the color red that you can only know when you actually experience red. Any good account of omniscience needs to take this into account. R. T. Mullins puts this point as follows:

> God must have experiential knowledge as well. For example, when God creates the universe, there is something that it is like for God to experience creating a universe out of nothing. God's experiential knowledge grows as He freely exercises His power and brings about new states of affairs into existence. God comes to know what it is like to experience His creatures for the first time, and this experiential knowledge is not reducible to God's propositional knowledge.[9]

Of course, prior to creation, God had ideas of the things he would create in his mind. Having prefect knowledge of his ideas, God would know what it would be like to be His creatures. Their origin grounded in the activity of the divine mind, creatures owe their existence to the way and the manner in which God thinks about them. God's manner of knowing is eternal, and God's knowledge is not propositional. It follows that God had eternal nonpropositional knowledge of the world prior to creating it. That is, before the world began to exist, God has eternally known it in His own mind. Because all times are present to God eternally, we don't see why God, then, cannot possess experiential knowledge of all things.

Now, it could be such that Classical Theism is not incompatible with experiential knowledge simpliciter, but perhaps there is specific type of experiential knowledge that the God of Classical Theism couldn't possess. For example, one might object that God wouldn't know what it is like to sin, or what have you. But there are ways around this sort of objection. One could reply that for God to lack experiential knowledge of this sort isn't a problem at all, for God to have this or that bit of knowledge would involve his having some sort of imperfection, and God lacks no perfection. Moreover, knowledge by experience is inferior to knowledge of essences and realties, which God fully has. Alternatively, one might argue that God has a certain pool of experiential knowledge from which he can perfectly extrapolate, or simulate, if you rather, all other bits of experiential knowledge.

What about emotions? Can God possess knowledge as it relates to experiencing different types of emotions? According to Mullins, "an emotion is a mental state that involves an evaluation that has a positive or negative affect."[10] Now, the doctrine of impassibility doesn't preclude God from having emotions, it just entails that God's creatures can't affect God's emotions in any positive or negative way. So, it could be such that God has emotional knowledge as He has been experiencing emotions or something like emotions for all eternity.

But what about the emotion of empathy? In order for subject S to display empathy, S needs to be aware of another subject, S*. Perhaps one is convinced that an omniscient Being would know what it is like to be in another subject's position. Mullins, once again, summarizes this point well:

Empathy is an epistemic state that one achieves. In particular, empathy is a kind of experiential knowledge of other persons. This epistemic state involves both cognitive and affective features. This epistemic state is distinct from the disposition, power, or capacity that one has to achieve a state of empathy. Empathy is achieved when one is consciously aware of how another person feels, and what it is like for them to feel that way.[11]

Must God rely on His creation in order to sympathize with another subject? For example, perhaps the Classical Theist also accepts the Christian doctrine of the Trinity. Couldn't such a Classical Theist say that one person in the Godhead has empathy for another person who exists in the Godhead? This seems like a reasonable response. However, for our purposes, it isn't fully adequate. For, clearly, it isn't a response that all Classical Theists could give, and, as promised, this book is supposed to synthesis Classical Theism simpliciter with Buddhism, not Christianity. Even so, the move has some weight. And we take it that other but functionally similar and exclusively Jewish or Islamic moves might be made here.

Moreover, wouldn't the Classical Theist still struggle with accounting for how God could have knowledge of what it is like to be a certain member of His creation? As Thomas Nagel famously argued, humans can't properly imagine what it would be like to experience the world by means of echolocation as bats do.[12] We lack the kinds of conscious experiences that enable us to know what it would like to be a bat. Being creatures, humans and bats are more similar to one another than either is to God. That suggests the surprising result that humans are in a better position to know what it would be like to be a bat than what it would be like to be God! Nevertheless, as hard as it might be, apparently, humans can empathize, to some degree, with bats who suffer on account of being stuck in a cave without food or water. Adding to the worry, wouldn't it be impossible for God to have empathy for particular members of any species given that, His own creation cannot affect Him? If so, would this mean that Tyler has empathy for his wife when God doesn't? Perhaps Tyler can know something—namely what it is like to be his wife—that God doesn't know.

Again, the Christian Classical Theist has an interesting response. The Christian can postulate the incarnation as a way for God to have empathy. God does know what it is like to be Tyler's wife because God took on human flesh. He suffered physical pain, felt hunger, and felt exhausted at various times. He can relate to Tyler's wife then, when she goes through physical pain, feels hunger, and feels *exhausted* (emphasis on exhaustion given that she is a mother of five young children). Of course, at least from our human point of view, it would still mean that there was a time when God didn't know what it was like to be like His creatures. So, this still seems to be a forceful objection. Naturally, Jewish and Islamic Classical Theists won't accept this response, for they do not accept the doctrine of the Incarnation. But insofar as God incarnating is logically possible, all non-Christian Classical Theists should acknowledge that this argument has at least some weight.

We think the best response the Classical Theist can give, and one that is open to all Classical Theists, Abrahamic or otherwise, is that God knows what it is like to be His creatures because His creatures owe their existence to the activity of God's own mind. God knows His creatures insofar as God knows Himself.[13] So, God knows exactly what it is like to be Tyler's wife, since she has been an eternal thought of His. In fact, this makes it such that God knows more about Tyler's wife than Tyler does as only God knows His own mind in a comprehensible way. So, while God can know what it is like to be a creature, could you say that God would lack knowledge with respect to what it is like to suffer? We now move to respond to this objection more fully.

Objection III: Objection from Love

Engaging with Eleanor Stump's work, Mullins argues that the God of Classical Theism cannot love. For one reason, love requires closeness and closeness cannot occur with another subject unless one knows what it is like to suffer as that subject.[14] Mullins states, "The first reason that the impassible God cannot satisfy the conditions for mutual closeness is because the impassible God cannot comprehend what it is like to suffer, and thus cannot comprehend what it is like to be Sally in her suffering."[15] Mullins, however, deals with a possible response. Call the response the Five Minutes Ago Response:

> STORY: Imagine that the universe popped into existence only five minutes ago. The universe came into existence with all of the appearance of age, including a whole host of memories and psychological states, etc. that lead the inhabitants of the universe to believe that it is in fact 13.5 billion years old. Imagine that Bill finds himself in this universe with the distinct memory of having his foot caught in a bear trap 15 years ago. The memory of this experience does not cause Bill any pain or discomfort at present. However, Bill does understand what it is like to experience having his foot caught in a bear trap.[16]

So, Bill could know what it's like to feel pain, even if he had never experienced pain. Similarly, couldn't God know what it's like to suffer even though He has never suffered? Could He, for example, have an idea of His creature going through hardship and, by knowing His own mind intimately, know how creatures would feel and react? Mullins doesn't think so, as he thinks God isn't in the same situation as Bill. We can say that Bill knows what it's like to suffer even though he has never suffered because Bill possesses the property of being able to suffer. However, God doesn't have the ability to suffer. So, the analogy developed doesn't work.[17] But, what is Bill's ability to suffer doing here? What makes it such that this information is relevant for explaining why Bill understands suffering and yet God cannot? This isn't clear.

Let's say that Bill doesn't possess the ability to suffer. For example, we might say that Bill is part of a newly discovered alien race called the Spockians. The Spockians don't have unpleasant mental states. Still,

Spockians are brilliant creatures. They can understand, in an abstract way, what suffering is like without actually having to experience it. Perhaps they invent a machine that allows them to understand what it's like to have an unpleasant state without actually having an unpleasant state. Couldn't we say Bill lacks the ability to suffer but still knows what it is like to suffer, at least to a sufficient degree such that he is able to genuinely love a woman from the human race? Perhaps this much may be granted. But Mullins may object that, just like the case of Mary, there is something one learns about suffering that you don't know without actually suffering yourself. You can be an expert on the philosophy of suffering, but, if you haven't actually suffered yourself, you are still missing some nonpropositional knowledge, namely, experiencing that suffering for yourself firsthand.

In response, one could first ask Mullins if God has always known what it is like to suffer. If so, then it seems like one would be committed to the view that God's existence *sans* creation is imperfect. God would have experienced suffering even before humans ever came into existence. If Mullins says no, then it appears that God wasn't always omniscient, as without creation there is still a thisness to suffering and God would not possess it.

Moreover, one could argue that God will never know what it is like to sin or know what it is like to be a creature, but as explained above, this doesn't count against omniscience. And, if nonpropositional knowledge of what it is like to sin or what it is like to be a creature doesn't count against God's omniscient, then His lacking nonpropositional knowledge relating to suffering shouldn't count against His omniscience either. Of course, one might argue that God does know what it is like to sin or to be a creature, given that He knows His own mind.

So far, we have argued that God could be impassible and still love a subject. He either can know the subject and what it's like to suffer through knowing His own mind, or we can say that certain experiential knowledge is simply not required to be omniscient. We now move to engage the fourth objection from William Abraham.[18]

Objection IV: Determinism

William Abraham argues that Classical Theists must endorse a problematic view of human freedom:

> [G]iven the way in which Neo-Thomists unpack the language of causality and dependence as applied to human action, there is an obvious problem in understanding what it is for God to directly bring about all human actions and how this generalization is to be squared with the reality of sinful human actions ... The claim sounds familiar. It appears to be a theological version of the compatibilism common among those who attempt to reconcile a supposedly scientific view of the universe where everything is determined including human actions, with the intuitively attractive claim that human actions are free because they are done voluntarily. Free actions are those that are caused in a certain way, that is, not by coercion, but inwardly by the dispositions, beliefs, motives, reasons, and desires of an agent. Thus understood, determinism and free will are compatible ... there is, of course, an immediate problem. What are we to make of the evil actions of human agents? If all human actions are directly brought about by God, then the "all" here, if it means anything, means that the evil acts of human agents are also brought about by God. It is hard to think of a more disastrous theological consequence for the vision of divine agency and divine action offered by the Neo-Thomist.[19]

So, would a Classical Theist be committed to determinism and a problematic view of divine causality and human evil? Not necessarily. W. Matthews Grant argues that the view that God causes all things is consistent with libertarianism. Explicating the doctrine of universal causality, Grant states the following:

According to the doctrine of divine universal causality, God is the source and cause of all being other than himself. The doctrine does not hold that God is the only cause. Still, it maintains that whatever is going on, including the genuine causal activities of things besides God, is an effect of God, the First Cause. Since human actions are beings and goings-on distinct from God, it follows according to this doctrine that they too are caused by God.[20]

Following Robert Kane, Grant states that, "A 'libertarian' view is one that affirms free will and that sees freedom as requiring that there be indeterminism at some relevant point in the process that produces a free act."[21] In contrast with defining libertarianism, again, following Kane, Grant argues that determinism should be defined as follows:

An event ... is determined when there are conditions obtaining earlier (such as the decrees of fate or the foreordaining acts of God or antecedent causes plus laws of nature) whose occurrence is a sufficient condition for the occurrence of the event. In other words, it must be the case that, if these earlier determining conditions obtain, then the determined event will occur.[22]

This leads Grant to conclude that, "An act is free in the libertarian sense if and only if the act is performed by its agent without there being any logically sufficient condition or cause of the action prior to the action itself."[23]

Following O'Connor, Grant gives two models of Divine Action:

Intrinsic model:
(a) God.
(b) A.
(c) Some real, intrinsic property, feature, or state of God in virtue of which God causes A, and which state would be different were God not causing A.
(d) The cause–effect relation between God and A.[24]

Extrinsic model:

(a) God.

(b) E.

(d) The cause–effect relation between God and E.[25]

Grant argues that if we accept an extrinsic model of Divine causation, we can endorse both libertarianism and Divine universal causality. As Grant puts it, "There might have been any number of different contingent orders, and in each such case, the contingent reality would have causally depended on God. Yet God Himself would have been intrinsically the same."[26] On this view, when God causes a world to exist, there is no change in God. The property *that God causes world W to exist* and the property *that God causes W* to exist* are relational, or Cambridge properties; such properties are extrinsic to God's nature, not intrinsic.

Our actions, then, can be seen as co-actualizing the effects that come about. And, since God causing E or God causing E* are not antecedently determining a creature's actions, we can say that the creature has libertarian freedom insofar as described above. We can say that while God causes a subject S to perform action A, there's nothing within God that is different from the world where God doesn't cause S to perform A. And in both cases, S has libertarian freedom. S is free, and God doesn't have malicious motivations which determine S's actions. The Thomistic conception of God doesn't entail a problematic view of divine action and human freedom and it doesn't entail determinism. Having now explicated Abraham's objection, we return to Mullin's work once more.

Objection V: Modal Collapse

Mullins has argued that the doctrine of simplicity can be shown to be false by way of developing a *reductio ad absurdum*. Mullins argues that divine simplicity necessitates a modal collapse:

Does divine simplicity entail a modal collapse? Yes. There are multiple ways to setup the modal collapse argument, and elsewhere I have defended several ways to do this. ... The simplest way is as follows. On divine simplicity God's essence is identical to His existence. Also, God's one simple act is identical to His essence/existence. God's act of creation is identical to this one simple act, and so identical to God's essence/existence. God exists of absolute necessity. So His act of creation is of absolute necessity since it is identical to His essence/existence.[27]

In response to this, Chris Tomaszewski first reformulates the argument in schematic form:

1. Necessarily, God exists.
2. God is identical to God's act of creation.
3. Necessarily, God's act of creation exists.[28]

Tomaszewski then decisively shows that the modal collapse argument is invalid. Tomaszewski correctly points out that proponents of the modal collapse argument commit a modal fallacy:

> Fortunately for the proponent of DDS, the argument from modal collapse is facially invalid, and indeed commits a fallacy that has been well-known since at least Quine (1953, ch. 8). It substitutes "God's act of creation" for "God" in to a modal context (within the scope of a necessity operator, to be exact), but as Quine teaches us, modal contexts are referentially opaque, which means that substitution into them does not generally preserve the truth of the sentence into which such a substitution has been made. To use Quine's own well-known example, while it is necessarily true that 8 is greater than 7, and it is true that the number of planets = 8, it is false that the number of planets is necessarily greater than 7.[29]

And, in this case, we should once again think that substitution does not preserve the truth of the relevant propositions. Classical Theists of the Thomistic stripe argue that *God's creating the world* is a Cambridge property and not a real property intrinsic to God.[30] Go back to the discussion in the last section where we argued that God causing everything is compatible with libertarian freedom. There we argued that, with respect to God, intrinsically, there is no difference between God in world[1] where S does A and God in world[2] where S does not do A. Even though S does something different in the two worlds, God is intrinsically identical in both worlds. While creatures enter into a real relationship with God, this relation is one way, as it were. That is to say, whether and whatsoever God creates, God remains intrinsically identical. Moreover, God only has a logical relationship with respect to differences between possible worlds and the world that actually God creates. Therefore, we see no reason to think that the substitution in question preserves the truth and because of this, what lies at the heart of Mullins's objection should be rejected. Having now dealt with these five objections, we move to consider one larger response that the Classical Theist can give when it comes to not only the aforementioned objections, but, most other objections as well.

Paradox as Theology

A paradox is an apparent contradiction that can be resolved by further reflection. James Anderson argues that Christians should see the doctrines of the incarnation (that the second person of the trinity, the Son, took on human flesh and obtained a human nature) and trinity as paradoxical doctrines rather than doctrines that articulate genuine contradictions.[31] For Anderson, it's irrational to affirm a contradiction but there are plenty of times where it is rational to affirm a paradox. Specifically, it is rational to affirm a paradox when the paradox is merely an apparent contradiction which is the result of an unarticulated equivocation (or what he calls MACRUE). Anderson gives various examples of when it's rational for one to affirm a paradox. Our favorite example goes as follows:

> [C]onsider the case of Harry, a Christian layman who has been invited by a friend to attend a lecture given by an eminent Continental theologian. Due to a combination of factors—a previous late night, the stuffiness of the lecture theatre, the monotony of the speaker's voice—Harry's attention drifts in and out during the course of the presentation. At one point, he hears the following claim: (B1) God's kingdom has arrived. Soon afterwards, he dozes off—only to awaken to catch this second claim: (B2) God's kingdom has not arrived. Harry's immediate thought is that the lecturer has flatly contradicted himself. Still, being a charitable chap by nature, and working on the assumption that an eminent Continental theologian would be unlikely to exhibit such flagrant illogicality, he quickly concludes that the speaker has in mind a distinction according to which God's kingdom has arrived in one sense but has not arrived in another sense. Having tuned out for most of the lecture, Harry is unable to say just what distinction is operative here, but nonetheless he is justified in believing that some distinction is operative and therefore that this is a MACRUE.[32]

In this case, there is clearly a sense in which the Kingdom of God is *here* and a sense in which the Kingdom of God is *not here*. There is an unarticulated equivocation going on and it is beyond Harry's ken to recognize where the equivocation lies. Nonetheless, Harry seems rational in trusting that the Kingdom of God is both here in some sense and not here in some other sense. It would seem rather foolish to question the esteemed theologian given that Harry isn't even a professional theologian.

For Anderson, as long as the belief is formed in the right way, the belief can be warranted. Anderson is a proper functionalist. Proper functionalism, again, is the following theory of warrant:

S's belief that P is warranted, iff …

1. The belief in question is formed by way of cognitive faculties that are properly functioning.
2. The cognitive faculties in question are aimed at the production of true beliefs.
3. The design plan is a good one. That is, when a belief is formed by way of truth-aimed cognitive proper function in the sort of environment for which the cognitive faculties in question were designed, there is a high objective probability that the resulting belief is true.
4. The belief is formed in the sort of environment for which the cognitive faculties in question were designed.[33]

In the case of Harry, Harry's belief that *the kingdom of God is here* has warrant since it was produced with the proper functionalist constraints being in place. Similarly, his belief that *the kingdom of God is not here* has warrant since it too was produced with the proper functionalist constraints being in place. Finally, assuming that Harry's conclusion that there is an unarticulated equivocation is the result of the proper function constraints being in place, Harry's belief that there is an unarticulated equivocation would be warranted.

Anderson argues that similarly, a Christian can be warranted in thinking that God can be one in essence and yet fully exist in each person of the trinity or that Jesus can be both truly God and truly man. Any attempt to derive a contradiction from these doctrines can be met with a claim that there is an unarticulated equivocation, which makes it rational to continue holding to the doctrine. Once again, as argued for in the last chapter, we don't think this move is *ad hoc*. To paraphrase Isaiah 55:8-9, God's thoughts are not like our thoughts, and his ways are not our ways. God is completely other. He is, as Paul Tillich puts it, "being-itself, beyond essence and existence."[34] Quoting Pseudo-Dionysius, Aquinas writes, "God … is not there: he is beyond what is there."[35] Naturally, while Jewish and Muslim Classical Theists don't accept the doctrine of the Trinity, it needn't be the case that they deny making this move has as least some force, for it seems to us that nothing forces them to say making this move is logically impossible. And that the doctrine of the Trinity is logically possible (or at least granted for the sake of argument to be so) is all we need for make our point about unarticulated equivocation. At any rate, our main point, that God's thoughts are beyond our thoughts, is equally acceptable to all Abrahamic and Non-Abrahamic Classical Theists.

Having now defended Classical Theism, we have motivated our readers to take seriously the claim that robust theism is compatible with Mere Buddhism. This concludes the first section of the book. Now, we move to discussing ethics and soteriology.

Buddhist Ethics and Theistic Ethics:
A Synthesis

Having defended and explicated the metaphysics of Classical Theism, we now move to synthesize the ethical systems that are generally assumed within the Abrahamic traditions with those ethical systems associated with Buddhist traditions. In order to do this, we first will give a short primer on Buddhism and ethics. Then, we will move to survey typical ethical theories associated with the Abrahamic traditions. Having done as much, we will offer a way to synthesize the various ethical systems.

Buddhism and Ethics

The Eightfold Path offers enlightenment for those who have right views, right intention, right speech, right action, right livelihood, right effort, right mindfulness, and right concentration. While there is a heavy emphasis in the Buddhist tradition on acting in an appropriate manner, it isn't clear what ethical systems are *necessitated* from the core tenets of Buddhism. As Maria Heim puts it, "There is a general consensus in the field of Buddhist studies that Buddhist thinkers did not offer systematic theories justifying moral principles in this way, though their texts everywhere explore moral psychology, exhort moral behavior, posit moral rules and norms, and explore virtue and high moral ideals."[1]

Of course, this hasn't stopped scholars from categorizing Buddhist ethics with well-known Western ethical systems. Some have cataloged

Buddhist ethics under the label of virtue or Aristotelian ethics. Others have argued that Buddhist ethics are really consequentialist in nature.[2] This is because Buddhist ethics are tied to getting the right result, that is, to reach enlightenment.[3] A subject should perform a particular action not because the action is intrinsically good *per se*, but because it leads to the end of suffering. Garfield puts it in the following way:

> Buddhist moral assessment and reasoning hence explicitly takes into account a number of dimensions of action. We cannot characterize a particular action as good or evil simpliciter in this framework, nor can we enumerate out obligations of permissions. Instead we examine the states of character reflected by and consequent to our intentions, our words, our motor acts, and their consequences.[4]

Of course, the goal isn't to merely diminish suffering in your life, as you aren't a distinct self. According to the interdependence thesis, "every event and every phenomenon is causally and constitutively dependent upon countless other phenomenon."[5] The boundaries and distinctions we see "are regarded as best conventional and relatively insignificant, and at worst deeply illusory."[6]

This can especially be seen in Santideva's *How to Lead an Awakened Life*. Heim summarizes:

> As a Mahayana thinker, Santideva aims not at the path of purification to achieve individual liberation of an arhat (as in the case of Buddhaghosa), but at this much grander and exalted ideal of saving all beings. Thus, as we consider Santideva's ethical thought, we will be concerned with questions of altruism and universal compassion, and challenging issues of self-sacrifice and radically altruistic ethical ideas that are constitutive of this higher vision.[7]

While previous Buddhist writings have merely emphasized The Eightfold Path, Santideva's work emphasizes the necessity to move beyond your suffering to end the suffering of all. Once again, however, it isn't obvious what ethical theory is espoused in Santideva's work. Some have interpreted it as an Aristotelian account and others as consequentialist one.[8] Garfield isn't keen on attempts to characterize Buddhist ethics in Western categories. Garfield states that " ... Buddhist moral theory is neither purely consequentialist nor purely areteic nor purely deontological. Elements of each kind of evaluation are present, but there is no overarching concern for a unified form of moral assessment."[9]

One important feature of Buddhist ethics that hasn't been discussed thus far is the concept of karma.[10] Briefly, karma is the consequences of action.[11] The idea being that the bundle of experiences which I am reduced to today has an effect on the interdependent bundle of experiences that will exist momentarily tomorrow. If the current bundle of experiences today helps to remove suffering from the world, then the causally related bundle of experiences that will exist tomorrow will suffer less. Burton puts it best:

> Buddhism typically rejects this view [the view of the self] because what we conventionally refer to as the 'self' is actually a complex conglomeration of causally connected impermanent events. Thus the person that I am today is a cluster of mental and physical events that is not the same as the person that I was yesterday, last year, or in a previous life and is not the same as the person I will be tomorrow, next year of in a future. Nevertheless, the person I am today is causally connected, often in very important and close ways to the person I was in the past and the person I will be in the future.[12]

We now have a motivation to avoid wrong actions. If we fail to live a life that is selfless and giving, then, conventionally speaking, the person who I will be tomorrow will suffer the consequences. In order to reduce the suffering tomorrow, I must act righteously today.

The Ethics of Abraham

Divine Command Theory

Traditionally, when theists articulate a moral ethical theory, they incorporate, to at least some degree, a divine command theory.[13] Divine command theory is, roughly, the theory that postulates that God's commands ground our moral obligations.[14] Classical Theists typically argue that the doctrine of simplicity entails that God is identical to goodness itself. Thus, while God's commands ground moral obligations, goodness itself is grounded in God's essence. This, of course, avoids the famous dilemma given in Plato's *Euthyphro*.[15] God's commands don't determine the good, rather God is the good. His commands merely determine our duties.

Obviously, there isn't much in the Buddhist literature that would seem to identify goodness with God or our moral duties with God's commandments. Nonetheless, there are theists who defend virtue theories[16] and consequentialist theories.[17] It is to these theories that we now turn.

Virtue Theory and Consequentialism

Utilitarianism is the standard consequentialist theory in ethics. Utilitarianism is the thesis that we should do those actions that bring about the greatest happiness for the greatest amount of people. Typically, theists who reject utilitarianism point to cruel and wicked scenarios that would be obligatory given utilitarianism. For example, one can imagine a world where ninety-nine percent of the population achieves happiness by way developing sophisticated ways to torture and eventually kill one percent of the population. Utilitarianism seems to render the ninety-nine percent's genocidal actions morally justified. This result seems obviously incompatible with Classical Theism. However, it is possible to show how a Theistic Utilitarian moral theory would rule out this apparent obligation to perform cruel and wicked actions.

For example, take Boethius's account of perfect happiness.[18] Similar to how God just is identical to goodness itself, for Boethius, God is also identical perfect happiness. Perfect happiness, then, cannot be affected by actions or decisions on earth; it is immutable. Boethius seems to suggest that humans can be happy by knowing God and by living a virtuous life.[19] If this is so, then loving God by following His commandments seems to bring about the most happiness for the most people. Thus, from a Utilitarian point of view, following God's commands is justified not just because God commands them, but because following those commands is the best way to bring the good that God would have us enjoy, namely, our coming to be in perfect union with Himself. John Stuart Mill maintains that "some *kinds* of pleasure are more desirable and more valuable than others" and argues that the golden rule of Jesus of Nazareth captures completely the spirit of the ethics of utility: "To do as one would be done by, and to love one's neighbor as oneself, constitute the ideal perfection of utilitarian morality."[20] Thus, Utilitarianism and divine command theory are compatible.

Moreover, it seems like we could also synthesize virtue ethics with these views. For perhaps it's part of God's plans to bring about our happiness by way of our performing virtuous acts, and so God commands us to perform virtuous actions for our own happiness. This seems consistent with Aristotle's view that it is by developing virtue and having (and enjoying) certain external goods that one achieves *eudaimonia*, or flourishing, the highest good available to us. Granted, Aristotle's account of the highest good for humans is an objective account of happiness; that is, strictly speaking, he does not think that one must have and value certain subjective experiential states such pleasure for one to flourish. However, as Mill goes on to argue, happiness includes virtue, for only those who have cultivated moral virtue are in the best position to enjoy the subjective goods of pleasure.[21] This goes to show that it is possible that following God's commandments is the best way to develop the moral virtues the having of which is necessary for and brings about the most happiness for the most number of people.

The Synthesis

But, how is an ethical system that emphasizes cultivating virtue and doing those actions that enable enlightenment compatible with the above ethical theories? It could be that God wants His creation to be enlightened. Perhaps, God wants us to recognize the fleeting nature of our existence and to recognize how we depend on Him for our being. That is, to put the point in Buddhist terminology, perhaps God wants His creatures to know that, ultimately, all conditioned realities are empty of own being. Recognizing this will lead His creation to become detached from the things in the world and to fixate not on creation but rather on the one who is ultimate reality.

If this is the case, it seems like the commands that God would give would be such that, when followed, enable us to achieve enlightenment. God cares for His creation and wants what is best for them. He gives His creatures the commands that he knows will end suffering once and for all. Hence, this could be why The Eightfold Path reflects the Ten Commandments so well. Let's again look at The Eightfold Path in light of the Ten Commandments.

Reading these commandments in light of Buddhist teachings, we see that in the first commandment, God cares about humans having the right view about ultimate reality. You cannot have the view that there is anything more valuable than Being itself. You must put God

Table 1 Table Comparing The Eightfold Path to the Ten Commandments

The Eightfold Path	The Ten Commandments
1. Right View	1. You shall have no other gods before me …
2. Right Intention	2. You shall not take the name of the LORD your God in vain …
3. Right Speech	3. Remember the sabbath day, to keep it holy …
4. Right Action	4. Honor your father and your mother …
5. Right Livelihood	5. You shall not kill …
6. Right Effort	6. You shall not commit adultery …
7. Right Mindfulness	7. You shall not steal …
8. Right Concentration	8. You shall not bear false witness against your neighbor …
	9. You shall not covet your neighbor's house; you shall not covet your neighbor's wife,
	10. Or his manservant, or his maidservant, or his ox, or his ass, or anything that is your neighbor's.[22]

before all things. Making sure that one has the right view of reality will also lead one to being mindful of Ultimate Reality and to concentrate on what is true. There are, then, overlaps between the First Noble Truth and the First Commandment.

The Second and Third Commandments align also with the Third tenet of The Eightfold Path. The Second Commandment encourages one to avoid wrong speech while the Third Commandment encourages one to avoid making God's day an ordinary day. Both commandments attempt to prevent one from making God out to be just another common thing. We shouldn't carelessly use God's name and confuse God for something we experience every day. Similarly, when God does something extraordinary and stops His creative activity, we, too, should stand in awe of God's rest and treat the day He rests differently than the way we treat every other day. Whether it be when we utter God's name or we worship Him on a particular day, we need to beware of confusing Being itself with a mere thing.

The next five commandments concern avoiding wrong actions. We should avoid dishonoring our family, we should also avoid murder, adultery, stealing, and lying. When we do these actions, we bring about conflict and pain. Not just for us but also for those who we are connected to. Doing such actions prevents us from loving our neighbor as our self.

The last two commandments relate to having a right heart. We shouldn't have inordinate desire for what isn't ours. When we are overcome by inordinate desire for things which we consider not our own, we not only cease to appreciate and enjoy the things that we have, we are a step away from envy and covetousness, and we also forget that all things are impermanent and we lose sight of the sense in which we are already connected to those things.

There are also overlaps between The Ten Commandments and The Five Precepts of Buddhism, which derive from The Eightfold Path. The Five Precepts are:

1. I undertake the precept to refrain from harming living creatures.
2. I undertake the precept to refrain from taking what has not been given.
3. I undertake the precept to refrain from sexual immorality.
4. I undertake the precept to refrain from refrain from speaking falsely.
5. I undertake the precept to refrain from taking intoxicants.[23]

The following table illustrates that there are practical but significant overlaps between The Ten Commandments and The Five Precepts.

The First Precept prohibits killing humans and animals. In The Commentary on *The Vinaya Piṭaka*, we read that committing murder is serious enough to warrant being cast out of the Buddhist community: "Whatever monk should intentionally deprive a human

Table 2 Table Comparing the Five Precepts to the Ten Commandments

The Five Precepts	The Ten Commandments
	1. You shall have no other gods before me ...
	2. You shall not take the name of the LORD your God in vain ...
	3. Remember the sabbath day, to keep it holy ...
	4. Honor your father and your mother ...
1. I undertake the precept to refrain from harming living creatures.	5. You shall not kill ...
1. I undertake the precept to refrain from harming living creatures; 3. I undertake the precept to refrain from sexual immorality.	6. You shall not commit adultery ...
1. I undertake the precept to refrain from harming living creatures. 2. I undertake the precept to refrain from taking what has not been given.	7. You shall not steal ...
4. I undertake the precept to refrain from refrain from speaking falsely.	8. You shall not bear false witness against your neighbor ...
	9. You shall not covet your neighbor's house; you shall not covet your neighbor's wife,
	10. Or his manservant, or his maidservant, or his ox, or his ass, or anything that is your neighbor's.[24]

being of life ... or should incite (anyone) to death: he is also defeated, he is not in communion."[25] Adultery is contrary to The Third Precept, that we should avoid engaging in activities that involve the misuse of the senses. And so, in *The Sutta-Nipāta*, we find the following caution against adultery: "Not to be contented with one's own wife but to be seen with prostitutes or the wives of others—this is a cause of one's downfall."[26] Stealing and lying, ways in which we cause harm to others, are collectively prohibited by The First Precept and individually prohibited by The Second and Fourth Precepts.

Reconciling Karma?

So far we've argued that the ethical considerations found within the Buddhist literature are compatible with the ethical systems endorsed by Classical Theists. God could want us to understand that ultimately, all reality, understood in terms of things, is empty of permanent and independent phenomena. Only God, transcending the reality of things, is truly permanent and independent. Therefore, via His commands, God calls us to form the right sort of character that leads to the consequence of becoming enlightened. There is no tension between divine command theory and the consequentialist and virtue considerations discussed by Buddhists. However, as discussed above, it would be wrong to jettison the doctrine of karma from Buddhist ethics. Perhaps the doctrine of karma is really what is in conflict with the Abrahamic traditions.

Now, there are at least two different ways to understand how karma works. There is a supernatural view and a more reductive or naturalistic view. In understanding the supernatural view, imagine there exists somewhere (perhaps in the heavens) a scale that keeps track of all of your good and bad actions. At the end of your life, if you had more good actions, you will have a more prosperous life in your next incarnation. If, however, you performed more bad actions than good ones, you might be reincarnated into a powerless and desolate human being, perhaps even something worse. On the supernatural view, there is a cosmic reality where our actions are counted and deliver to us positive or negative repercussions. Given that Classical Theists generally deny reincarnation, most Classical Theists will be put off by this account of karma.

On a reductive reading, the doctrine of karma is merely the belief that actions have consequences. Those actions that are in line with The Eightfold Path will lead to furthering the bundle of experiences that currently make you up, to reaching enlightenment. When we don't follow The Eightfold Path, we become ignorantly attached to a false reality. We take that which is impermanent as permanent and that which is interdependent as independent. We become stuck in a cycle of pain. Burton summarizes the reductive view:

> Proponents of naturalized karma point out that intentional actions have an impact on the agent's character in this life, with good actions improving one's character and bad actions detrimentally affecting one's character. For instance, an intention to hurt others harms the agent's character by making him or her a more hateful sort of person, who is more likely to act from a hateful motivation in the future; the intention to help others benefits the agent's character by making him or her a more benevolent sort of person, who is more likely to act with a kindly intention.[27]

The naturalistic account of karma is also compatible with the idea of being able to share one's karma with another human being. We share the consequence of our actions not by some transcendent or cosmic scale that dictates how our next life will be, but rather by way of all things being interconnected. Every action that I take will have an impact on someone else. And the impact I have on someone will impact yet another. In this way, when I do good actions, I help my neighbor become one step closer to enlightenment. When I commit bad actions, I help prevent my brother and sister from reaching nirvana.

All that has been stated seems compatible with Classical Theism. None of this denies the existence of a God who will judge each person according to their deeds. Nor does the belief in karma entail the doctrine of reincarnation. Theism can fit quite well with a reductive account of karma. In fact, the doctrine of karma seems well situated within a theistic framework. For, on theism, it seems like we will be held even more accountable for our actions. Perhaps God will hold us responsible for all of the good and bad karma that we share.

Nevertheless, what good does showing that the ethical systems of Buddhism and Classical Theism are compatible do, if, their soteriologies are shown to be in conflict? It's one thing to make sense of karma on Classical Theism, but it is a whole other thing to make sense of Nirvana with a worldview that espouses an eschatology that involves a resurrection. We now move to synthesis Buddhist soteriology with various soteriologies found within the Abrahamic traditions.

Buddhist Soteriology and
the God of Abraham

So far we have shown how the central metaphysics underlining the Buddhist tradition are compatible with the metaphysics assumed in Classical Theism. We then moved to argue that you can understand the general ethical systems espoused in the Abrahamic traditions as compatible with the ethical philosophy typically endorsed in the Buddhist tradition. In this chapter, we plan to argue that the soteriology espoused in the Abrahamic traditions can be seen as consistent with the soteriology espoused by what we call Mere Buddhism. In order to do this, we will first briefly survey the soteriological systems in Judaism, Christianity, and then Islam. After this, we give a brief survey on how Buddhist philosophers generally understand salvation. Finally, we conclude by synthesizing the overall soteriological system endorsed by the Abrahamic traditions with the Buddhist tradition. We now move to discussing the soteriology of Judaism.

Judaism

Central to Judaism is the Torah, the first five books of the Hebrew Bible. In the Torah, we read about God creating the first humans and informing them that they are to take dominion over the earth and that they should be fruitful and multiply. We see quickly the fall of man and the rise of sin. The world becomes so polluted with sin that God sees it necessary to bring about a flood to wash the sin away. God ends up calling an elderly man, who will later be known as Abraham, to leave his current location and to follow God. God promises to make Abraham the father of many nations. Abraham's grandson, Jacob, ends up having twelve sons. His sons move to Egypt during a famine. It is here where Jacob's progeny, now known as the Hebrews, would expand by leaps and bounds. There comes a day, however, when a ruler doesn't take to Abraham's descendants and forces them into slavery. Eventually, God raises up a prophet, Moses, who through God's intervention, leads his people out of Egypt and into a land that will later be called Israel. The rest of the Torah speaks of various laws for how the Hebrews—now known as Israelites—should conduct themselves in worship and in government. In total, God gives 613 commandments in the Torah.

The Torah recounts how God entered into a special covenant with the Israelites. And, those who trust in God's grace and enter into this special relationship with God can also become part of the chosen people.[1] Those who remain in the covenant, trusting in God and keeping His commandments, will be part of the resurrection of the just. While most of the tribes of Israel have disappeared, those in the tribe of Judah have kept intact their identity and are now better known as the Jewish people. But what if you aren't part of the Jewish people? Are you destined for damnation? Based on early passages in the Torah, Jewish scholars typically endorse the view that gentiles can be made right with God if they keep the Noahide laws. One well-known Jewish institution summarizes them as follows:

1. **Do not profane God's Oneness in any way.** Acknowledge that there is a single God who cares about what we are doing and desires that we take care of His world.
2. **Do not curse your Creator.** No matter how angry you may be, do not take it out verbally against your Creator.
3. **Do not murder.** The value of human life cannot be measured. To destroy a single human life is to destroy the entire world— because, for that person, the world has ceased to exist. It follows

that by sustaining a single human life, you are sustaining an entire universe.

4. **Do not eat a limb of a living animal.** Respect the life of all God's creatures. As intelligent beings, we have a duty not to cause undue pain to other creatures.

5. **Do not steal.** Whatever benefits you receive in this world, make sure that none of them are at the unfair expense of someone else.

6. **Harness and channel the human libido.** Incest, adultery, rape, and homosexual relations are forbidden. The family unit is the foundation of human society. Sexuality is the fountain of life and so nothing is more holy than the sexual act. So, too, when abused, nothing can be more debasing and destructive to the human being.

7. **Establish courts of law and ensure justice in our world.** With every small act of justice, we are restoring harmony to our world, synchronizing it with a supernal order. That is why we must keep the laws established by our government for the country's stability and harmony.[2]

Ultimately, then, in Judaism, salvation relates to the deliverance from the consequences of sin and entering into a peaceful relationship with our Creator. There are different traditions within Judaism with respect to whether the resurrection of the body is central to salvation.[3] There are those who endorse what is known as Intellectualism, roughly, the view that while there will be a resurrection of the dead, resurrected bodies are not permanent. We will once again die. The resurrection merely happens to testify to God's power. It shows that God is powerful enough to even raise the dead to life. This is contrasted with the view known as Devotionalism. Those who advocate for Devotionalism argue that the resurrection is fundamental to the salvation story. The resurrection isn't merely an example of God's strength, but it's God's ultimate aim. God desires that humans possess permanent bodies that don't decay. Resurrecting the righteous to spend an eternity with God, argues the Devotionalist, is the end of our salvation.

Christianity

Christianity in some sense is an extension of Judaism. Saint Pope John Paul II is known for rightfully recognizing the Jews as the Christians' "elder brother." Christians believe that not only did Jesus keep the Torah perfectly, but Jesus is the fulfillment of the Torah. And those in union with Jesus are credited with Jesus's Torah keeping. Believers are seen as keeping Torah perfectly. Moreover, in union with Jesus, Christians now are said to observe the Torah in a unique way. For example, Christians observe the command to keep the Passover Sedar, or feast, by way of partaking in the Eucharist. While various Christian denominations have different interpretations of the Theology of the Eucharist, of central importance to all is the crucifixion of Jesus. Jesus is understood to be the new Passover lamb. Similarly, many branches of Christianity, including the Catholic Church and the Eastern Orthodox Church, believe that Jesus is the fulfillment of the other Jewish feast days and celebrate these feast days through the Christian liturgy. Many of the rules and commands given to the Israelites have contemporary application to us by understanding them allegorically. For example, God's command to the Israelites to wipe out the Canaanites can now be understood as a command for Christians (Israelites) to wipe out sin (Canaanites).

To be saved, then, one must be tied to Jesus and his death, burial, resurrection, and kingship. A subject can be tied to Jesus through the sacrament of baptism. Baptism allows one to enter into a relationship with Christ and to receive His Torah keeping righteousness. And as the Christian works out their salvation through fear and trembling, through the means of partaking in the sacraments, a Christian actually becomes righteous. Through union with Jesus, Christians are able to do good works by the power of the Holy Spirit. And, on judgment day, God will judge us by these works. Those who were spiritually faithful to God's law will participate in the resurrection of the just.

Christianity can best be summarized by the Nicene Creed:

For a summary of Christian belief, see the Nicene Creed which states the following:

> We believe in one God,
> the Father, the Almighty,
> Maker of all that is, seen and unseen.
> We believe in one Lord, Jesus Christ,
> the only Son of God,
> eternally begotten of the Father,
> God from God, Light from Light,
> true God from true God,
> begotten, not made, consubstantial
> of one Being with the Father.
> Through him all things were made.
> For us men and for our salvation
> he came down from heaven,
> and by the Holy Spirit was incarnate of the Virgin Mary,
> and became man.
> For our sake he was crucified under Pontius Pilate;
> he suffered death and was buried.
> On the third day he rose again
> in accordance with the Scriptures;
> he ascended into heaven
> and is seated at the right hand of the Father.
> He will come again in glory to judge the living and the dead,
> and his kingdom will have no end.
> We believe in the Holy Spirit, the Lord, the giver of life,
> who proceeds from the Father and the Son.
> With the Father and the Son he is worshipped and glorified.
> He has spoken through the Prophets.

We believe in one holy catholic and apostolic Church.
We acknowledge one baptism for the forgiveness of sins.
We look for the resurrection of the dead,
and the life of the world to come. Amen.[4]

As the Creed hints at, Christians are Devotionalists about the resurrection of the body. The resurrection of the just is the main event of the eschaton; it is God's ultimate plan. The hope in Christianity is not merely that we go to an immaterial realm known as heaven by way of being a disembodied soul. Rather, the hope is to be delivered from the consequences of sin by God resurrecting our bodies and bringing peace on earth. We are to dwell with God through Jesus for all eternity.

What happens to those who don't have a relationship with Jesus? Christianity teaches that those who do not enter into a relationship with Jesus are not seen as righteous. They have failed to keep God's laws and commandments and will be judged accordingly. Traditional Christian theology teaches that the unrighteous will experience hell for all eternity. One need not understand hell by the literal description of fire and an outer darkness. Nonetheless, the idea is that hell is a place of great spiritual suffering and it's to be avoided.

Of course, some Christians are optimistic about who will be part of the resurrection of the just. For example, some Christians think that one can be implicitly trusting in Jesus and his Torah keeping. For instance, Catholics maintain that salvation comes from Christ and that there are those who, "through no fault of their own, do not believe that, but nevertheless seek God with a sincere heart, being moved by grace, try to do his will as it is known through the dictates of their conscience … too achieve eternal salvation."[5] Explicating this view, Karl Rahner writes:

Anonymous Christianity means that a person lives in the grace of God and attains salvation outside of explicitly constituted Christianity … Let us say, a Buddhist monk … who, because he follows his conscience, attains salvation and lives in the grace of God; of him I must say that he is an anonymous Christian; if not, I would have to presuppose that there is a genuine path to salvation that really attains that goal, but that simply has nothing to do with Jesus Christ. But I cannot do that. And so, if I hold if everyone depends upon Jesus Christ for salvation, and if at the same time I hold that many live in the world who have not expressly recognized Jesus Christ, then there remains in my opinion nothing else but to take up this postulate of an anonymous Christianity.[6]

In summary, according to the Christian view, salvation relates to being delivered from sin and its consequences through the person and work of Jesus. Catholics (and some non-Catholics, too[7]) affirm that one needn't explicitly confess Jesus as their messiah and king. Instead, by trusting in the true, the good, and the beautiful, one can be said to be trusting in Jesus without realizing it. In this way, some even hope that all will ultimately be saved.[8]

Islam

Similar to how Christians see themselves in line with the tradition of Judaism, Muslims see themselves in line with both Judaism and Christianity. However, Muslims believe that the Jewish and Christian Holy Scriptures that we currently possess are now corrupted. If these Scriptures were not corrupted, Jews would recognize that Muhammad is a prophet like Moses and Christians wouldn't believe that Jesus is divine or that he died for the sins of the world. Instead, God raised up the prophet Muhammad to fix the errors in these corrupted revelations. The Quran is seen as the final revelation from God. And through it and the broader Islamic tradition, we find out that if one wants the greatest assurance of entering paradise, one should commit oneself to The Five Pillars of Islam:

1. The Confession (or *shahadah*): In order to become a Muslim, one must wholeheartedly assert "There is no god but God and Muhammad is the messenger of God."
2. Prayer: In Islam, Muslims are commanded to pray five times a day (dawn, noon, afternoon, evening, and night).
3. Alms Giving: Muslims are commanded to give out of their own income.
4. Fasting: Muslims are commanded to fast during the month of Ramadan.
5. The Pilgrimage: Muslims are commanded to make a journey to Mecca and walk around the Kaaba seven times.[9]

Of course, following The Five Pillars of Islam does not guarantee one eternal life. A person's salvation is ultimately depended on God's decision:

> Everyone is facilitated for what was created for him. Deeds are judged as they are at the end of life. Those who are blessed are blessed by the decree of Allah, and those who are damned are damned by the decree of Allah. Thus, take extreme caution from that type of investigation, thinking, and insinuation. For Allah the Exalted has hidden the knowledge of providence from His creatures and has prohibited them from seeking it, as said by Allah the Exalted in His Book, 'He will not be questioned about what He does, but they will be questioned,' (21:23). Whoever asks why He did something has rejected the judgment of the Book, and whoever rejects the judgment of the Book is among the unbelievers ... We hope that Allah will pardon the good-doers among the believers and admit them into Paradise by His mercy. We cannot guarantee it for them and we cannot testify that they will be in Paradise. We seek forgiveness for the sinful, we fear for them, yet we do not despair over them. Those who commit major sins among the nation of Muhammad, peace and blessings be upon him, may be in Hellfire but will not reside there forever, if they die while they are monotheists, even if they have not repented. After they meet

Allah knowing faith, they are subject to His will and His judgment. If He wills, He will forgive them and pardon them by His grace, as mentioned by the Almighty in His book, 'He forgives whatever is less than idolatry for whomever He wills, (4:116) If He wills, He will punish them in Hellfire by His justice. Thereafter, He will bring them out of Hellfire by His mercy and the intercession of intercessors among those obedient to Him, then raise them to Paradise. This is because Allah the Exalted is the ally of those who recognize Him and He will not deal with them in the two abodes as if they were the people who rejected Him, who failed to follow His guidance and did not earn His guardianship. O Allah, Guardian of Islam and its people, keep us firmly upon Islam until we meet You. We have faith in the Resurrection and the recompense for actions on the Day of Resurrection, the presentation of deeds, the reckoning, and the reading of the book of deeds, the reward and punishment, the Bridge over Hell (*al-ṣiraṭ*), and the Scale (*al-mīzan*). Paradise and Hellfire are two creations that never end, nor perish. For Allah the Exalted created Paradise and Hellfire before the rest of creation, then He created people for them. Whoever He wills enters Paradise due to His grace, and whoever He wills enters Hellfire due to His justice. Everyone acts in accordance with what is decreed for him, becoming that for which he was created. This is our religion and what we take as our creed, inwardly and outwardly.[10]

So, according to Islam, there is a resurrection of the dead. Some will go to heaven and others to hell. Ultimately, God decides who will enter into everlasting righteousness, and, who will experience the fires of hell. Nonetheless, there appears to be an understanding that the way to up the likelihood of getting into heaven is by way of faithfully following God and his messenger, Muhammad. Having briefly surveyed the soteriological systems within the Abrahamic traditions, we now move to discuss soteriology according to the Buddhist tradition.

Buddhism

In the Abrahamic religions, salvation is a matter of being in union with God and enjoying his presence in the afterlife. Common to Judaism, Christianity, and Islam is the idea that believers are resurrected to enjoy an eternity with God. Compared to that of the Abrahamic religions, the Buddhist conception of salvation is minimalistic. While more traditional Buddhists affirm reincarnation, any existence in this world is not an end to be desired, for suffering (*dukkha*) is an ever-present feature of our worldly existence. The Buddhist soteriological aim, therefore, is the elimination of suffering in this life and final release from *samsara*, the cycle of birth, death, and rebirth. In short, salvation is not a destination or place, but a matter of achieving release, which requires enlightenment. In addition to this, the more traditional forms of Buddhism teach that it is possible for a person to achieve this enlightenment by means of their own effort. This is in contrast to the Abrahamic notion that humans need to be reconciled to God and that they aren't able to do that apart from God's activity and grace.

To understand salvation in Buddhism, we must understand the nature of the human predicament and what to do about it. In Chapter Four we discussed the core elements of Buddhism with a focus on Buddhist Ethics. In this chapter we take another look at the Four Noble Truths and revisit The Eightfold Path and consider them from a soteriological standpoint.

The First Noble Truth is that life contains "suffering." The Second Noble Truth is that *dukkha* is caused or conditioned by desire (*taṇhā*), or "thirst." The idea is that for anything you care to pick, the conditions for its existence are dependent on some other thing, and you won't find any unconditioned thing on which all things depend. (This is the doctrine of *pratītya-samupāda*, or co-dependent origination, which states that everything is dependent on everything else.) The Third

Noble Truth is that there is a path to *nirvāna* (literally, blowing out or extinction), liberation from the continuity of *dukkha*. *Nirvāna* is "the end of the series of unsatisfactory existences [*dukkha*] through the extinction of the fires of possessiveness, antagonism, and delusion that generate rebirth-causing actions."[11] Because *nirvāna* is a post-mortem state, not a place or thing, and because experiences of it are ineffable, the tradition is extremely reluctant to say anything positive about *nirvāna*. But they do affirm that those who achieve *nirvāna* have extinguished the three poisons of ignorance/delusion, attachment/greed, and aversion/hatred that drive the wheel of *samsara*. This leads to well-known metaphorical description of nirvāna: If our existence is analogous to that of the flame of a burning candle, then *nirvāna* is the blowing out of that flame. The Fourth Noble Truth is that there is a path to *nirvāna*, The Eightfold Path. The Eightfold Path, again, is stated as follows: right views, right thoughts or resolve (wisdom), right speech, right action, right livelihood, right effort (morality), right mindfulness, and right concentration or meditation. It is worthwhile to go through and discuss each.

Having *right views* is basically coming to accept the first three Noble Truths. Having *right thoughts* is matter of developing attitudes of freedom from desire, friendliness, and compassion; abandoning hatred, sensual desire, and abstaining from causing injury (*ahimsa*). *Right speech* involves not telling lies, avoiding divisive speech, harsh speech, i.e., hateful or abusive language, and frivolous talk, e.g., idle chatter or gossip. *Right action* amounts to avoiding killing, stealing, inappropriate sexual conduct and the like. *Right livelihood* involves not engaging in an occupation that is causes harm to humans or animals. For instance, right livelihood precludes one from taking up certain professions, such as those of butcher, arms dealer, or abortionist. *Right effort* involves mental cultivation, transforming one's mind by replacing negative thoughts with positive ones. Right mindfulness is a matter of developing constant awareness of one's body, feelings, moods and mental states, and one's thoughts, as well as the elimination of hindrances, such as sensual desire, sloth, worry, anxiety, and the like. Right concentration involves developing mental clarity and calm by concentrating the mind through meditational exercises.[12]

Achieving *nirvāna* involves more than mere intellectual assent, it requires daily practice. In earlier Buddhist traditions, salvation was understood to be obtained for oneself by oneself. No savior figure, not even the Buddha himself, is necessary for achieving the salvation of *nirvāna*. We see this teaching clearly in the *Mahāparinibbāna Sutta* (*The Discourse on the Great Passing Away*), which records an interaction between Buddha and Ānada, his most devout follower. Ānada, worried about what would happen to the *sangha*, the order of monks, after the Buddha's death. He was concerned how they could make progress toward enlightenment without his comforting presence in their lives, as well as the need for instruction about daily practice and other logistical matters. The Buddha tells Ānada that he held nothing back from them when he was with them and with his passing he and the other monks have everything they'll need. He then says:

> Ānada, you must be your own lamps, be your own refuges. Take refuge in nothing outside yourselves. Hold firm to the truth [i.e., The Four Noble Truths] as a lamp and a refuge, and do not look for refuge to anything besides yourselves.[13]

He then tells him how to go about doing that.

> A monk becomes his own lamp and refuge by continually looking on his body, feelings, perceptions, moods, and ideas in such a manner that he conquers the cravings and depressions of ordinary men and is always strenuous, self-possessed, and collected in mind. Whoever among the monks does this, either now or when I am dead, if he is anxious to learn, he will reach the summit [i.e., *nirvāna*].[14]

The early Buddhist view that salvation is possible only by one's own effort remains a central part of *Theravada* Buddhism. As Buddhism developed, particularly as it spread into China and Japan, Buddhists maintained that achieving salvation did not depend solely on one's own effort, and this led to the formation of various *Mahāyāna* Buddhist traditions. On salvation in the *Mahāyāna* traditions, Maier writes:

> Mahāyāna teaching emphasizes "compassion," which involves aiding people in all areas of their lives, even though such aid does not lead directly toward *nirvāna*. In Mahāyāna Buddhism, salvation does not depend solely upon one's own effort. Good merit can be transferred from one person to others. No one can exist by himself physically and spiritually. Mahāyānists regard the egoistic approach to salvation as unrealistic, impossible, and unethical … Instead of seeking *Nirvāna* just for oneself in order to become an *arhat* [an enlightened one], the disciple of Mahāyāna Buddhism aims to become a *bodhisattva*, a celestial being that postpones his own entrance into *parinirvāna* (final extinction) in order to help other humans attain it. Such a person swears not to enter *Nirvāna* until he fulfills this noble mission … The *bodhisattva* beings help humans work out their liberation. Therefore, a *bodhisattva* ("Buddha-to-be") rather than an *arahat* becomes the ideal one seeks to achieve the religious discipline. The bodhisattva beings help humans work out their salvation. In the process of obtaining this goal, one realizes that all beings can benefit each other because they all depend upon each other. Salvation depends on the help of others. A good teacher can assist students on the path of salvation.[15]

The Mere Buddhist could have an affinity with either earlier Buddhist traditions or later Buddhist traditions as it relates to the roles of grace and merit. This needn't bother us too much for our broader purposes in this volume. Having now explicated how soteriology is broadly understood in the Buddhist tradition, we move to synthesize it with the Abrahamic traditions.

Synthesis

While the minimalist notion of salvation in Buddhism may lead one to think that it can't be reconciled with an Abrahamic concept of salvation, there is room for overlap here. At the root of the Buddhist soteriological system is the view that one can reach *nirvāna* by way of eliminating desire that leads to suffering. The Abrahamic religions also recognize that desire can lead to suffering and offers a way to avoid it. According to the Abrahamic religions, humans act as if various things—such as people, objects, and money—are Ultimate Reality. We spend a life trying to obtain status and wealth, when in reality, these things exist aren't the Ultimate Reality. As the explication of these traditions make clear, once we recognize that we and our selfish desires are not a part of Ultimate Reality, we lose our self-centered disposition. We get lost in Being; we escape suffering by right realization. Doesn't this broadly fit with what we have discussed in this chapter?

To summarize what is essential to a Mere Buddhist's soteriology, it's helpful to recall what Garfield considers to be essential as discussed in Chapter One. Garfield again states that "The origin of *dukkha* is in primal confusion about the fundamental nature of reality, and so its cure is at bottom a reorientation toward ontology and an awakening (*bodhi*) to the actual nature of existence."[16] And specifically addressing salvation he states, "The elimination (*nirvāna*), or at least the substantial reduction of *dukkha* through such reorientation, is possible."[17] What we have sketched is completely compatible with this. The origin of suffering is found in confusing what is ultimate with what is not. And escaping suffering is achieved by a right orientation toward reality.

We can then add that the Buddhist who also identifies as a Classical Theist can rightly believe that part of the process of how she escapes suffering is by way of God resurrecting her body once she dies. And in their resurrected body, she can focus on God and see Ultimate Reality for how it actually is. Classical Theists refer to this as the Beatific Vision.

None of this goes against how Garfield characterizes suffering or salvation in the Mere Buddhist tradition. Because of this, we fail to see why the Abrahamic traditions and a Mere Buddhist tradition are necessarily in conflict. Having now engaged the various metaphysical, ethical, and soteriological tenets found within Mere Buddhism, we think we showed how a Buddhist can be a Classical Theist. Showing how a Buddhist can be a Classical Theist is an accomplishment in itself. However, one might be worried that one can't take both Mere Buddhism and Classical Theism seriously and also avoid pluralism about religious belief. It's to this concern that we now turn.

Pluralism: Part One

Having now synthesized Classical Theism with Buddhism, we now entertain the question of whether both the Classical Theist's and the Buddhist's religious experience can be seen as veridical, that is, as mapping onto reality. This chapter will focus on John Hick's argument for religious pluralism. While we eventually argue that the Classical Theist can take the Buddhist's religious experience as veridical, in this chapter, we entertain Hick's argument for religious pluralism as an objection to our view. Though Hick sees Buddhist religious experience as on par with theistic religious experience insofar as both experiences are not veridical, we nonetheless want to argue that both types of religious experience can be seen as veridical. Hick wouldn't be pleased.

Utilizing the work of Alvin Plantinga, William Alston, and William Lane Craig, we argue that Hick's view that all religious experience is nonveridical is unfounded. This will lead to the next chapter where we offer up a new model for how Classical Theists should perceive the religious experiences reported by their Buddhist counterparts. This model will be immune to the critiques provided in this chapter to Hick's own model. While this book is written from a Mere Classical Theist point of view, we present our critiques to Hick's views from a Christian perspective. This could be done from an Islamic or Hindu perspective as well. However, we will be doing this from the perspective that we think can best respond to Hick's arguments.

Hick's Pluralism and the Equal Weight Theory

Hick has developed the most sophisticated account of religious pluralism. Hick utilizes a Kantian distinction between the noumenal and phenomenal realms to help articulate his view. Hick argues that religious practitioners of the main faiths of the world come to form beliefs about God, or The Real, through their own tradition-dependent concepts. The religious practitioners do not know The Real as it actually is or what could be understood as the noumenal level; instead they know The Real insofar as how they perceive The Real, that's to say at the phenomenal level:

> Kant distinguished between the noumenon and phenomenon, or between a *Ding an sich* and that thing as it appears to human consciousness ... In this strand of Kant's thought—not the only strand, but the one which I am seeking to press into service in the epistemology of religion—the noumenal world exists independently of our perception of it and the phenomenal world is that same world as it appears to our human consciousness ... I want to say that the noumenal Real is experienced and thought by different human mentalities, forming and formed by different religious traditions, as the range of gods and absolutes which the phenomenology of religion reports.[1]

Motivating his view seems to be an implicit commitment to the conciliatory view about epistemic peer disagreement. Roughly, a proponent of the conciliatory view thinks that when there are two epistemic peers who disagree about a proposition P, the subjects should become agnostic about P or, at least, decrease their confidence in P. Behind the conciliatory view is something like the equal-weight theory, which states the following:

> The Equal Weight View: In cases of peer disagreement, one should give equal weight to the opinion of a peer and to one's own opinion.[2]

An argument for the Equal Weight theory can be seen in the following syllogism:

1. It is unreasonable to hold to one's views in the face of disagreement since one would need some positive reason to privilege one's views over one's opponent['s views].
2. No such reason is available since the disagreeing parties are epistemic peers and have access to the same evidence.
3. Therefore, one should give equal weight to the opinion of an epistemic peer and to one's own opinion in the case of epistemic disagreement.[3]

We can picture a scenario where a Christian, an orthodox Jew, a Muslim, a Hindu, and a Buddhist all sit together at a table. Each one comes to believe that their counterparts are roughly just as intelligent and just as well read. According to the equal weight theory, each religious practitioner, upon recognizing that there exist epistemic peers with whom they disagree, should no longer endorse their creedal religious beliefs. Each proponent has had religious experiences within their own creedal tradition, and each knows the other's arguments for why one should endorse their particular creedal tradition. Hick thinks under these conditions, the only rational thing to do is to become agnostic about the nature of ultimate reality. While the ethics espoused by each tradition are essentially the same, the metaphysical views can be understood very differently. There is no justifying reason as to why one should prefer one creedal tradition to another.

Plantinga's Response to Pluralism

Plantinga, however, is not impressed by Hick's reasoning. Plantinga invites the reader to imagine a scenario where two subjects disagree about a specific moral proposition. For example, S might believe that it is wrong to lie about her colleagues in order to advance her career, while S* might believe that it is permissible to do so. We can imagine that S and S* are good friends. Perhaps they have exchanged various arguments for their views, but they can never come to an agreement. Is S within her rights to continue on in her belief that it is immoral to lie about her colleagues? Has she violated any epistemic duties? Is she being merely hardheaded if she continues in her belief? No.[4]

Plantinga, again, is a proper functionalist. Plantinga believes that a subject's belief will be warranted as long as it is the result of properly functioning cognitive faculties that are successfully aimed at the production of true beliefs. For Plantinga, then, as long as the belief in question is produced in a way that accords with proper function constraints, the belief will have warrant, even in light of epistemic peer disagreement. Plantinga endorses what elsewhere McNabb calls the Classic Plantingian Approach:

> CPR: S's belief that p can deflect defeater D if S still believes p on the reflection of D and p is the product of properly functioning faculties which are successfully aimed at truth and there is a high objective probability that the belief produced under these conditions would be true.[5]

Moreover, as Plantinga points out, it's likely that the Christian won't think that she is an epistemic peer with everyone she sits with at the table. Even if each member of the table is roughly just as smart and each person has read the same material, the Christian will likely think that she has something going for her that the others do not, namely, that she has a faculty that is putting her in touch with true beliefs about God and His activities and the others lack this properly working faculty.[6] She might even think that sin has played a role in why the people at the table each believe so differently. But the Spirit of God has reversed the noetic effects of sin for her. In this case, you can even endorse a conciliatory view but still deny that the Christian in question must give equal weight to the other religious practitioners as they are not her epistemic peers. Hick's reasoning for his pluralism seems weak and unconvincing, especially if one denies the conciliatory view.

An Argument from the Resurrection

William Alston gives a further reason as to why the Christian could be within her epistemic right in endorsing her specific creedal tradition while rejecting others. Alston alludes to there being a historical argument for privileging Christian belief. While Alston never gives such an argument, we think William Lane Craig's argument for the resurrection of Jesus is very persuasive. After we articulate and defend Craig's argument, we then apply a similar methodology to the events surrounding Fátima, and argue that there are good reasons for thinking that Mary performed what is known as the miracle of the sun. If these arguments are sound, we will have additional reasons for why we should reject pluralism, at least, the Hickian kind. The resurrection of Jesus and the apparition of Mary add to the probability that Christianity, specifically Catholicism, is true.

Following the majority of New Testament scholars, Craig sets out to discuss and argue for the following:

Fact (1): Jesus died by crucifixion.

Fact (2): Jesus was buried in a tomb by a member of the Sanhedrin, Joseph of Arimathea.

Fact (3): The tomb became empty.

Fact (4): The disciples believed that they had encountered the risen Jesus.[7]

(1) is affirmed because it is attested to by multiple early sources. For example, Josephus[8] and Tacitus,[9] two respected ancient historians, both talk about Jesus's death. (2) is made plausible by the fact that it's unlikely that the early Christians would have claimed, if it were not

so, that a member of the Sanhedrin named Joseph, buried the body of Jesus. Not only did the early Christians name the specific member of the Sanhedrin but they went on to state where the member of the Sanhedrin was from. There were only seventy-one persons on the Sanhedrin Council and such members were well-known.[10] If Joseph of Arimathea was a fictionalized character, later Jewish authorities could have easily refuted the early Christian's claim.

(3) is made plausible by way of utilizing the criterion of embarrassment. We understand this criterion as follows:

> CE: If subject S states that P, S has nothing to gain by stating that P, and if it is embarrassing for S to affirm P, then, all things being equal, that S affirms P increases the likelihood of P being true.

We know that in the first century, unfortunately, the testimony of women didn't hold much weight. If you are trying to start a cult, it seems unlikely that you would mention that women were the first to see the empty tomb, at least, in their context.[11] This would be embarrassing and unlikely to be in the Gospel texts unless it happened.

Finally, (4) is affirmed in part, because there are early reliable testimonies of Jesus appearing not just to individual disciples but to groups.[12] Moreover, there is good historical reason to think that some of the disciples were tortured and died for their faith.[13] It is one thing to die for a lie that you believe to be true; it's another thing to die for something you made up. It seems unlikely then that the disciples knew that Jesus didn't rise from the dead but nonetheless, kept preaching this proposition as true, even when it meant their persecution and sometimes death.

Are these facts evidence that Jesus really rose from the dead? One standard naturalistic account of the aforementioned facts is that the disciples merely hallucinated. Perhaps, in a scrambled mental state, having just lost who they believed to be the messiah, the disciples hallucinated that Jesus rose from the dead. This is unlikely, however. As Michael Licona lays out in his work, the theory that the group hallucinated together and all saw the same thing is simply implausible given what we know from contemporary psychology.[14] Lastly, the hallucination theory still doesn't explain the empty tomb.

Given the above discussion, if one already has good reasons to believe in God, then it seems like there is a powerful reason to affirm the resurrection hypothesis. And, if there is good reason to prefer Christianity to other religious traditions in light of a nonexperiential argument, then it seems Alston is right: there is positive epistemic reason to prefer Christianity over other religious traditions.

Hick, of course, denies the resurrection hypothesis. Hick thinks that the "so-called" resurrection appearances are related to the visions of light that persons sometimes see during near-death experiences.[15] Hick thinks that the disciples must have hallucinated some sort of light and mistook it for Jesus. While this goes against the clear accounts of the resurrection in the Gospels, Hick thinks that the Gospels were not authored by eyewitnesses and were in fact anonymous.[16] The Gospel accounts were latter fabrications of the disciples' experience of the risen Jesus.

In responding to Hick, there is no reason to believe that the Gospels were anonymous and not written by eyewitnesses. Every full manuscript that we have of Matthew, Mark, Luke, and John has the traditional name associated with the Gospel attached to it.[17] Moreover, there are internal clues in the Gospels that point to there being eyewitness sources behind some of its content. For example, in Mark 15:21, the author lists the sons of Simon of Cyrene as Alexander and Rufus. Why would the author of Mark do this unless he understood that the community he was writing to knew of Alexander and Rufus?[18] The audience understood that the events recorded in the Gospels had living eyewitnesses still around. The Gospels were not written to a culture completely separated from the actual events.

In fact, as Bauckham points out, Mark likely mentions Alexander and Rufus as they were the sources behind Mark's statement about Simon.[19]

Finally, the four facts discussed above do not rely on the Gospel accounts being reliable. The Gospels could overall be unreliable and yet the points made would still stand. Hick, as far as we know, never addressed this point.

Perhaps, the reader assumes that a practitioner of another religious tradition could just as easily make a persuasive argument for their religious tradition. Zain Ali, for example, argues that there is a powerful argument for Islam. You wouldn't expect, so says Ali, for the Arab world to be united, for the Qur'an to transform the Arabic language, and for the Qur'an to display true moral exemplars, such as Abraham's great grandson, Joseph, on the hypothesis that God did not commission the Prophet Muhammad to bring about the Qur'an.[20] *Contra* Ali, we don't think that this sort of argument is on the same epistemic grounds as the argument from the resurrection. First, it seems like you could argue that Christianity united all of Europe and the Americas, and, transformed various languages, such as German and English, through the translation of the New Testament. Moreover, the depiction of a flawless and supernatural being like Jesus as depicted by the New Testament seems like an even greater exemplar than Joseph. Are we to take all of this as evidence for the New Testament being God's inspired and uncorrupted Word? Presumably, Ali would not be inclined to say as much. Moreover, even if Ali is right, Islam would have to deny the historical consensus that Jesus died on the cross, and it would fail to make sense of the disciples' sincere belief in the resurrection. Thus, even if there is some positive evidence for Islam, it wouldn't follow that it is epistemically on par with Christianity. We think Alston is right; Christianity is in a different epistemic position than other religious traditions. In fact, we think there is a similar argument for Catholicism. On that note, we move to give an argument that McNabb and Joseph Blado have recently developed. Much of what follows is taken from their paper, "Mary and Fátima: A Modest C-Inductive Argument for Catholicism."[21]

The Miracle of Fátima

In the early 1900s, Christianity in Portugal was predicted to become extinct. Seminaries were closing and very few people were joining the priesthood.[22] Portugal, from a Catholic's point of view, needed a major revival. The reported apparitions of Mary to the children in Fátima and the so-called Miracle of the Sun, helped meet this need.

Broken down, there were a total of nine appearances to the three shepherd children involved in the events at Fátima—the first three of which were appearances of the guardian angel of Portugal, and the latter six of which were of the Virgin Mary. During the three appearances of the guardian angel, the angel encouraged the children to fervently pray to the hearts of Jesus and Mary as the angels offered them the Eucharist. The angel proclaimed to them, "take and drink of the Body and Blood of Jesus Christ, horribly outraged by ungrateful men. Make reparation for their crimes and console your God."[23]

Soon afterwards, on May 13th, the Virgin Mary appears to the children for the first time. Mary tells them that she comes from Heaven, and that she wants to continue to meet them every thirteenth of each month for six months. During the following month, June 13th, Mary appears again and openly proclaims that one of the shepherd children, Lucia, will soon be alone (the others will die) and that she would have to spread a devotion to her Immaculate Heart.[24] During the third appearance, word of the Marian appearances had spread, and some two to three thousand people gathered at the site where Mary would appear to the children. When Mary appears, she shows the children a vision of hell and calls them once again to establish a devotion to the Immaculate Heart of Mary.

The fourth appearance (August the 13th) does not go as planned as the children's civil administrator intervenes and kidnaps the children until August 15th.[25] One by one the civil administrator takes the children into a room and threatens to kill them unless they share a secret which the children claimed the Virgin entrusted them with.[26] All three children, however, consistently keep to their testimony that the Virgin Mary had been appearing to them, thus, seemingly vindicating the sincerity of their beliefs. Mary again appears to the children after the incident on the 19th of that month and encourages them again to do penance for the sins of the world.[27]

The fifth appearance occurs on September the 13th, where Mary proclaims the importance of reciting the Rosary. The subsequent month, it rained all day prior to the appearance and up until the predicted appearance at noon. Around noon, the raining stopped, and the sun came out.[28] Here, most of those who were at Fátima at the time (roughly 50,000–100,000) saw something fantastic. The standard story is that the crowd, without pain, looked upon the sun (or something that looked like the sun) and saw the sun turn multiple colors and dance. It was widely reported that the sun ended up moving toward the crowd as if it were about to crash, and then right before it appeared like it was going to hit the earth, the sun returned to normal.[29] There is some disagreement about what exactly happened. For example, some of the witnesses debated whether the sun moved, and some claimed that they did not see anything at all.[30] Regardless, the vast majority seemed to agree that something unexplainable happened. It is also widely reported that while the crowds were still staring into the sky, their clothes became completely dry within minutes. Shocked by all of this, the common belief in Fátima was that a miracle had occurred. What followed was a robust Catholic revival throughout Portugal.

Alternative Explanations

We now move to engage the two most plausible naturalistic theories as to what happened at Fátima. First, there is what we call the Solar Retina theory. Roughly, the theory is that the people of Fátima experienced phenomena that can occur when one's retina is damaged by the sun. Stanley Jaki quotes Stöckl in describing how this damage leads to seeing the sun change colors and dance:

> When the sun is high in the sky it is dangerous to look at it even for a few seconds. When the sun is not so high, namely, when veils of clouds, or humidity and dust dominate more and more in the atmosphere and dampen the sunlight, one can for several minutes look at the sun, without damaging the eye. The following subjective effects may arise (I myself made that experiment several times): After almost a minute (the time varies according to the condition of the atmosphere and the momentary condition of the eyes) one thinks to see a dark blue disk in front of the sun (this is already a sign of the highly excited state of the retina). According to my experience ... the dark blue disk is somewhat smaller than the solar disk, so that the edge of that disk stands out as a ring beyond that dark blue disk. Then one has right away the impression that the solar disk rotates with great speed in one or the other direction.[31]

Monique Hope-Ross, Stephen Travers, and David Mooney studied four persons who, on their own initiative, decided to look at the sun to see if they could see Mary or perhaps repeat what was seen at Fátima.[32] Only one of the four persons was able to see the sun turn different colors and dance around and it took the one person looking at the sun at a favorable time of day for a few minutes intermittently. All four individuals were left with permanent eye damage. In addition to this, Auguste Meesen, a physicist at Catholic University of Louvain, tried this experiment. While he did not see the sun move in any way, he did see the sun change different colors.[33]

According to Ross, Travers, and Mooney, "the phenomena described is known as solar retinopathy and it is due to a combination of thermal and photochemical injury ... It is thought that solar retinopathy is caused by the photochemical effects of the short wavelengths in the visible spectrum at 400–500 nm, with some thermal enhancement from longer wavelengths in the infrared."[34] Could this be what happened to those observers at Fátima?

Perhaps. This theory, however, fails to explain several facts surrounding the events at Fátima. First, it fails to explain how the observers' clothes quickly became dry after the events had unfolded. Second, there appear to be reported witnesses who were not looking up toward the sun for a significant period of time, but nonetheless, saw the sun change colors and dance.[35] You wouldn't expect to find such witnesses on the hypothesis that the phenomena were merely produced from eye damage that results from prolonged observation of the sun. Third, this theory doesn't explain why the clear majority of observers were able to see the phenomena when it's common to look at the sun and not observe such an event. And fourth, it doesn't explain why the children of Fátima sincerely believed that they were coming into contact with Mary. It seems as if one would have to postulate an additional hallucination theory to make sense of their sincerity. Given all this, the Sola Retina Theory doesn't seem to hold up well in its ability to explain the facts.

We think the Meteorological Theory has more going for it. Jaki summarizes how irregularities in the atmosphere could be what was behind Fátima:

> The dashing of the image of the sun three times towards the earth may have been caused by a sudden temperature inversion. The latter can be surmised in the oppressive heat, registered by quite a few eyewitnesses, a condition certainly noteworthy in a day that was unusually cold a few hours earlier. The moving to right and left of the image of the sun, as produced by a lens of air full

of ice crystals, could be due to turbulence often present in a fast moving air. The combination of shear and temperature inversion could have propelled the lens of air along a curved path, such as an ellipse, on which still smaller circular turbulences could be superimposed. A shift in the position of ice-crystals in that lens of air could conceivably change the kind of refraction they produce in the air immediately surrounding them. This in turn can issue in the kind of phenomenon which appeared to the eyewitnesses as a firewheel projecting shafts of light of different color which in turn were reflected on those on the ground.[36]

On this theory, Jaki thinks the temperature inversion explains why the clothes dried up so quickly. This theory would also explain how there were witnesses who weren't looking up toward the sun for a significant period, but nonetheless, saw the image of sun change colors and dance. This of course is because there would have been real phenomena occurring in the sky. Third, it explains why most observers were able to see the same phenomena, when it's common to look at the sun and not observe the phenomena at Fátima.

However, the theory isn't without its problems. For example, a mere meteorological explanation does not explain why the children of Fátima *sincerely* believed that they were seeing Mary, and it still doesn't explain how the children were able to predict when the meteorological happening would occur. Of course, one wouldn't have these problems if Mary really did reveal herself to the children, and if God guided the meteorological happening to coincide with the children's predictions. Following Jaki, we endorse a Meteorological Theory in conjunction with the theory that God was behind the timing of the meteorological event and the Marian apparitions.

What about those who claimed to have seen nothing special occur? We don't have access to judge why it is the case that some claimed to have not seen anything or why some saw the sun change colors but not move. And we know that at least according to the New

Testament, in at least one case, one individual is reported as seeing a miracle while others around him do not (see Acts 9:7). We agree that this is a weakness in the theory proposed. However, as we have argued for, the alternatives seem to explain far less. Regardless of the theory one takes, it seems likely that there was something in the environment that either increased the likelihood of most members in the crowd seeing the phenomena discussed from retina damage, or, increased the likelihood of seeing an irregular meteorological event. On a minimalist view, the Miracle of Fátima is found in the children's ability to predict that some unusual event would occur at the exact place and time. Let the Miracle of Fátima be considered, *E*, evidence that can be explained. Would we expect *E* on the hypothesis that Catholicism is true (*CH*)? It seems like we would. And, it seems like we wouldn't expect *E* as much on -*CH*. So, we think the argument explicated here is a good historical argument that supports a specific religious tradition. Again, Alston's point against Hick is vindicated. There is yet, another, successful historical argument for Christianity, or in this case, specifically Catholicism.

Perhaps, one agrees that the argument developed here is successful; it nonetheless can be offset or made impotent by competing miracles that happen in anti-Catholic contexts, such as in Protestant churches that possess numerous zealous former Catholics. Assuming these miracles to be legitimate, some could see these miracles undercutting the argument from the Miracle of Fátima. Call this the Competing Miracles Argument (CMA).

We think CMA fails as we think we should expect competing miracle claims in anti-Catholic Protestant settings. To understand this intuition, consider the following thought experiment. Suppose that a man named Jerry has a daughter named Sophia. Jerry, being an extremely devout and dedicated Roman Catholic, raises Sophia in the Roman Catholic tradition. As Sophia grows older, Jerry—being the loving and kind father that he is—promises to Sophia that he would bail her out of any financial trouble if she ever fell into such a situation. Sophia begins to drift away from her father and eventually goes to college, graduates, and begins working a full-time job. As she works, she finds herself dialoguing with her co-workers who are primarily Evangelical Protestants. After much dialogue and discernment, Sophia decides ultimately to leave the Roman Catholic tradition to become a devout Protestant. Not only this, but Sophia's Evangelical Protestant friends influence her, so much so, that she becomes extremely anti-Roman Catholic. While her renewed faith somehow sparks a renewed interest in communicating with her father again, all is not well with Sophia. Sophia ends up losing her job after a couple of years working there and cannot seem to pay her monthly payments toward the debt she accrued from her college loans. She turns to her dad Jerry, the devout Roman Catholic, who, despite Sophia choosing to go against the tradition he raised (and intended) her to be in, nevertheless keeps his promise and pays off her monthly payments. Now, why could this not be the case with Protestants who call on the name of Jesus? Indeed, Jesus says time and time again that He will grant that which is asked of Him, "ask and it will be given to you; seek, and you will find; knock and it will be opened to you" (Matthew 7:7), and again He says "whatever you ask in my name, this I will do, that the Father may be glorified in the Son. If you ask me anything in my name, I will do it" (John 14:13–14). Thus, should we really be surprised that God answers His children when they call on His name?

Another modest response to the CMA objection is to say that the nature of the Fátima miracle is such that it distinctly points toward Catholicism, similar to how Jesus's resurrection points to Christianity. Indeed, consider the miracle of the resurrection relative to various miracles outside of Christianity. These miracles include spontaneous healings, monetary or financial support, and perhaps even changes in weather conditions. Although these miracles occur outside of Christianity, the fact that Jesus rose from the dead is a much more potent argument for Christianity over these various other religions since the nature of the miracle points toward a very specific religious tradition. Similarly, then, since Mary is very much a Catholic figure, so to speak, her appearance and miracle work—on average—points to the Catholic tradition over any other tradition.

Now, perhaps the Muslim or the orthodox Jew takes issue with what has been argued for. That's fine. As stated before, this book is meant to be an ecumenical one. We merely used the above discussion to illustrate how a committed religious practitioner could overcome Hick's objection. If the reader has qualms with these arguments and prefer other historical arguments for their respective religious traditions, they can replace the arguments offered here with those. As long as the reader has a better grasp as to how one could respond to Hick, we take it that the arguments discussed have served their purpose.

Conclusion

In this chapter, we first conveyed Hick's pluralism. Then, we argued against it. We argued that it assumes controversial epistemic views that some philosophers will not hold. We also argued that there exist arguments for the epistemic superiority of Christianity and even Catholicism, that don't exist for other religious traditions. Having now done all of this, in the next chapter we plan to advocate for a different model for understanding Buddhist religious experiences that is inclusive and doesn't yield ground to religious pluralism.

Pluralism: Part Two

In this chapter we argue that the Classical Theist's experiences of God and the Buddhist's religious experiences, specifically the experience of emptiness (*śūnyatā*), can both be seen as veridical.

Characterizing the Experience of Emptiness[1]

Crucial to our case is the claim that it is possible for both Classical Theists and Buddhists to have the same type of Buddhist experience of emptiness. While there are many Buddhist traditions that we could engage with, for our project, we focus on emptiness as it is understood in the Zen tradition broadly construed. While it would be interesting to show how it is possible for Buddhists to have specifically Jewish or Islamic religious experiences, we do not consider these possibilities at this juncture, as it is not essential to the success of the project of this book. For now, we will use the tradition we are most familiar with—the Christian tradition—to show how both Buddhist and Classical Theist religious experiences can be veridical.

Let's take John, a Buddhist of the Zen tradition, and Paul, a Classical Theist of the Christian and Thomistic tradition, as examples to help make our point. Both have practiced the Zen Buddhist sitting meditation, *zazen*, and as a result, both have had the same kind of religious experience of emptiness. Specifically, both have had the unmediated impression that all things are interconnected, impermanent, and empty of own-being (*svabhava-sunya*). It's not possible to express in words the nature of their experience;

nonetheless, we can gesture at what John and Paul have experienced. The aim of Zen meditation is enlightenment, or *satori*. Robert Wilkinson writes, "*satori* is direct apprehension of being-as-is" that "occurs when consciousness realizes a state of 'one thought.'"[2] Upon achieving *satori*, emptiness, is revealed: one has an unmediated impression or realization that all reality is *sunyata*—interconnected, impermanent, wholly undifferentiated (nondualistic), and void of own-being. Of course, this realization is not brought about by thinking through various arguments. It's rather achieved through practicing *zazen*. Upon having this experience, one is left with the impression of an impersonal, absolute reality to which none of our concepts and conceptual distinctions accurately apply. The experience has been conveyed as psychologically compelling, liberating, even joyful, an experience that involves a positive attitude toward all that is.[3] For the purposes of this chapter, what we care about is understanding the impression that reality is empty of own-being (*svabhava-sunya*). We refer to this impression as *sunyata* experience.

Perhaps you are already suspicious of *sunyata* experience. Maybe your worry can be summarized as follows: *Sunyata* experience leaves one with the impression of an impersonal, absolute reality to which none of our concepts and conceptual distinctions accurately apply, and yet, one applies to absolute reality the concept of *being something to which our concepts don't accurately apply*. There is an inconsistency here. This inconsistency might move someone to no longer take *sunyata* experience seriously. In response, note that while *sunyata* experience gives one the impression of an impersonal, absolute reality to which none of our concepts and conceptual distinctions rightly apply, *sunyata* experience is nonconceptual and cannot be accurately conveyed in conceptual terms. Nonetheless, we can help others have an idea of the experience by describing what the experience is like, by giving analogies. Recall that the Classical Theist is already committed to using analogical language when describing God. For the Classical

Theist, God's essence is incommunicable. In like manner, while we can't give a univocal linguistic account of *sunyata* experience, we are in a position to say what it is *not* like. Those who have had it can tell us when our concepts of it fail to represent it properly.

When Zen Buddhists claim that ultimate reality is empty of own-being, they are denying the *Abhidharma* Buddhist doctrine that the impermanence thesis does not apply to dharmas (roughly, objects of experience that can't be analyzed into simpler constituents). You will recall that we spoke about this doctrine earlier in Chapter One. John endorses the view that even the basic elements of experience are "empty of own-being" (*svabhava-sunya*). Moreover, he endorses the dependence thesis. All things are indeed connected and depend on one another. As we argued in Chapter One, to maintain that all things are empty of own-being is neither to affirm nor deny the existence of some ultimate reality above or beyond the basic elements of existence. As such, it follows that, for a Zen Buddhist such as John, having *sunyata* experience does not necessarily preclude him from also accepting Classical Theism.

Another potential obstacle is skepticism about how it could be that a Classical Theist has had *sunyata* experience. While this skepticism might seem *prima facie* interesting, upon further investigation, it is easy to address. Zen Buddhists have engaged in Christian meditative practices and Christians have engaged in Zen Buddhist religious practices. Representatives from both groups have reported having both Zen Buddhist and Christian religious experiences.[4] Some people, including Ruben L. F. Habito, identify as both a Christian and a Buddhist.[5] This goes to show that there are people who are in a position to have had Buddhist religious experiences, including *sunyata* experience, as well as religious experiences of the God of Classical Theism.

One may press the point further and argue that our attempt to discuss *sunyata* experience doesn't even get off the ground. Again, one may object that for those who accept that *sunyata* experience is beyond description to go on to use words to try to describe what having that kind of experience would be like is to attempt to perform a task that can only fail. We respond to this worry by employing the distinction between ultimate truth and conventional truth and distinguishing everyday experience from *sunyata* experience.[6]

Masao Abe argues that although Buddhists speak of everything as being empty, they do not deny that our everyday concepts and beliefs are absolutely inapplicable to reality. Rather, they mean to say that those concepts won't hold up under thorough examination. Here is a clear example: We will say that the sun rises or the sun sets, even though, strictly speaking, we know that talking this way doesn't accurately describe reality. In Buddhist terminology, from the standpoint of everyday experience, that the sun rises is a conventional truth. However, given what we know as citizens of the twenty-first century, "The sun rises" isn't an ultimate truth. As Masao Abe puts the point, "Conventionally, the sun rises; really, it does not. Conventionally, objects exist; really, they are empty."[7]

Conventional truth and ultimate truth are connected. According to Abe, "ultimate truth encompasses mundane life and validates its conventional meaning. The two truths theory is not intended to be a refutation of worldly, or conventional, truth in favor of ultimate truth, but rather it indicates the dynamic structure and interrelationship of the two truths."[8] Having made clear what conventional truths are, we are now in the position to make clear how we can talk about *sunyata* experience. We can use statements that are conventionally true to help move or point us in the direction of ultimate truth. In this case, we can make statements that get us close to understanding the ultimate truth of *sunyata*. Moreover, we can have conventional level experiences that lead us to experience ultimate reality for how it is.

Nishida makes intelligible *sunyata* experience by way of utilizing William James's notion of pure experience. While not the same experience, *sunyata* experience and pure experience are related. James affirms that pure experience is conceptually unmediated, direct perception.[9] On James's view, Joel Krueger writes:

> According to James, pure experience is the non-conceptual givenness of the aboriginal field of the immediate, a phenomenal field prior to the interpretive structures (and concomitantly, subject-object bifurcations or conceptual discriminations) that we subsequently impose upon it. Pure experience is prior to the reflexive thematizing of the cogito in language and thought ... pure experience is a pure *seeing* ... it simply bears mute witness to the world in all its 'blooming, buzzing confusion.'[10]

Pure experience is prior to all further experiences; all other cognitions are derived from it. Pure experience is unified, nondualistic, and beyond our cognitive grasping.[11] On pure experience, Nishida writes:

> To experience means to know facts just as they are, to know in accordance with facts by completely relinquishing one's own fabrications. What we usually refer to as experience is adulterated with some sort of thought, so *by pure experience I am referring to the state of experience just as it is without the least addition of deliberative discrimination.* The moment of seeing a color or hearing a sound, for example, is prior not only to the thought that the color or sound is the activity of an external object or that one is sensing it, but also to the judgment of what the color or sound might be. In this regard, *pure experience is identical with direct experience.* When one directly experiences one's own state of consciousness, there is not yet a subject or an object, and knowing and its object are completely unified. This is the most refined type of experience ... when one makes judgments about it, it ceases to be a pure experience. A truly pure experience ... is simply a present consciousness of facts just as they are.[12]

Utilizing Kantian terms, he writes, "from the standpoint of pure experience ... experience is not bound to such forms as time, space, and individual persons; rather these discriminations derive from an intuition that transcends them."[13] Nishida's thinking is an attempt to articulate into a Western Philosophical Framework what's behind *Mahāyāna* texts such as "*Nirvana* is *Samsara*,"[14] and "form is emptiness, emptiness is form."[15]

Characterizing the Intersection of Buddhist and Christian Religious Experience

We've said a lot about John's Buddhist experiences. Let us now turn our attention to explicating the religious experiences of Paul, a Classical Theist in the Thomistic Tradition. We do so with our eye on showing how it could be that Paul has not only these experiences, but also has *sunyata* religious experiences. We do not aim at giving a complete account of Paul's uniquely Christian and Thomistic beliefs. Our aim is to show how a subset of those beliefs allows for an intersection between his affirmation of Classical Theism and that of the Fundamental Metaphysical Theses of Buddhism.

Paul accepts what we will call the doctrine of the Godhead. The doctrine of the Godhead, at least how we are using it for this chapter, pertains to God as absolutely transcendent. We call this aspect of God the "far side" of God. This aspect of God is ultimately not communicable. The far side of God is what we think Christian mystics such as St. John of the Cross and Meister Eckhart have in mind when they say God can be known through a process called unknowing. In terminology reminiscent of Paul Tillich, Donald Mitchell argues that there is silence in the Godhead that can be experienced as "the ground of Being and beings."[16] On the other hand, Christians may consider the descriptions of God in Scripture to capture the "near side" of the triune God. Wolfhart Pannenberg puts it this way:

[A]bsolute reality does have a personal aspect as well as an impersonal one ... the Christian doctrine of the trinity involves both, the personal and the impersonal element, because the one "essence" the three persons share is not once more a person in its own right in addition to the Father, the Son, and Spirit. The one divine essence of Father, Son, and Spirit is suprapersonal. Not separate from the three persons, however, but exists only as it is manifest through Father, Son, and Spirit ... in their mutual relationships with one another ... in terms of a mutual perichoresis, or indwelling of the three.[17]

Recall our discussion in Chapter One. We argued that Classical Theists deny that we can speak about God and His creation univocally. The same is true for Paul, especially as he understands the Godhead. And this all seems consistent with not being able to understand God's essence. God is incomprehensible. As Pseudo-Dionysius states that, "We must not then dare to speak, or indeed to form any conception, of the hidden super-essential Godhead, except those things that are revealed to us from the Holy Scriptures."[18] Clarence Rolt nicknames Pseudo-Dionysius's view, "the doctrine of the Super-Essential Godhead." Roughly, the idea is that, "God is, in His ultimate Nature, Supra-Personal."[19]

Thomas Aquinas, following Pseudo-Dionysius, argues that we can't know God's essence because words cannot accurately express God's nature. Aquinas maintains that while God is perfect, His creatures are not. There is no apparent problem in holding to these two views unless one also holds, as Aquinas does, that we can only know God through His creatures. If we can only know the perfect through the imperfect, our knowledge of God will be imperfect. For reasons such as this, Aquinas thinks that words can "express God's substance and say something of what God really is, but represent him inadequately."[20]

Kenosis and Emptiness

In order to explicate the common ground between Paul and John, we bring to bear one of Paul's uniquely Christian belief, namely, that Jesus is the incarnate Son of God. According to the Chalcedonian model, Jesus is both God and man. There are various models that are advanced in an attempt to understand how Jesus could have a divine nature and a human nature. One controversial model is known as the kenotic model. Roughly, the kenotic model understands that the second person of the Trinity (who we call Jesus) emptied himself of those properties that are traditionally predicated to God, properties such as being all-powerful, when he took on a human nature. While we don't endorse the model here, we think this model can help elucidate the consistency between John and Paul's beliefs. The best support for the model is found in *Philippians* 2:5–8:

> Have the same attitude that Christ Jesus had. Although he was in the form of God and equal with God, he did not take advantage of this equality. Instead, he emptied himself by taking on the form of a servant, by becoming like other humans, by having a human appearance. He humbled himself by becoming obedient to the point of death, death on a cross.[21]

On one kenotic model, David Brown states that "roughly … God became human and subsequently became God again."[22] We want to distance ourselves from *this* articulation of the model as it seems to entail that Jesus was not God in essence. Instead, let's imagine that Paul accepts a version of the kenotic model that is explicitly consistent with the Chalcedonian model. On this model, Jesus, the second person of the Trinity, temporally forsook attributes often associated with divinity, and yet, always kept his divine nature. The kenotic model does not imply that the second person of the Trinity lost divinity, nor does it imply that Jesus was not divine.[23] In step with a

Chalcedonian model of kenosis, Ronald J. Feenstra, quoting Gottfried Thomasius, writes, "Omnipotence is no 'more' of the absolute power, omniscience is no enhancements of the immanent divine knowledge, omnipresence is no enhancement of the divine life. Thus, if the Son as man has given up these attributes, he lacks nothing which is essential for God to be God."[24]

Feenstra references various biblical texts to support his view. Specifically, he cites *Luke* 2:52 which reads that "Jesus increased in wisdom and stature." The clear indication of this passage is that Jesus, at least during his youth and adolescence, wasn't omniscient. To support the view that Jesus lacked omniscience as an adult, Feenstra cites *Matthew* 24:36, in which Jesus states that, "But of that day and hour knoweth no man, no, not even the angels of heaven, but My Father only." This passage can plausibly be read as Jesus affirming that there is something that he does not know. That this is so is, at least, *prima facie* in tension with the claim that Jesus is omniscient. However, passages such as these are intelligible and unsurprising on the kenotic model. That we find such passages in the Bible, therefore, can potentially count in favor of accepting the kenotic model.

Sunyata and Kenosis

The Kyoto school proponents, such as Nishida, Nishitani, and Abe, agree with Paul in thinking that *kenosis* is a fundamental theological doctrine. The Kyoto school would be pleased to hear that Christianity utilizes the concept of emptiness to make sense of ultimate reality. Hence, they will also agree with Paul that there is a sense in which God is empty. There is clearly fruitful ground to be had when *kenosis* takes center stage in ecumenical discussions. While there is time for a *kumbaya* moment, it is important to mention that there is a debate as to how *kenosis* or emptiness applies to God. The Kyoto proponents take themselves to be talking about the "far side" of ultimate reality (or Godhead) when discussing the God of Classical Theism. What drives that assumption is the belief that all Being is ultimately empty. If all Being is empty, then the personal aspect of God is ultimately empty, too. It follows that the claim that God is personal is a conventional truth. Moreover, on this view, each person of the Trinity must be self-emptying. There is ultimate *kenosis*.

Those in the Kyoto school understand the emptiness of *sunyata* to be ultimate truth. Thus they deny that it is an ultimate truth that God has a personal "near side." In contrast, Classical Theists may accept that God has both near and far sides; they may affirm that "near side" of God is the personal aspect of God and that the impersonal, or empty, aspect of God is the "far side."

We now have a clear way to understand how Buddhist religious experience and Theistic religious experience both can be veridical. Assuming that Classical Theism is true, we follow Paul in seeing that a Buddhist's religious experience is tapping into the "far side" of God, while the theist's religious experience maps on to the "near side" of God. On Paul's view, while both the Buddhist and the theist are coming into contact with ultimate reality, the theist's religious experience maps on to the more fundamental part of reality.

As we argued in Chapter One, Mere Buddhism neither affirms nor denies that there is anything that transcends this impersonal far side. A Buddhist who has *sunyata* experience of the sort described here may understand its metaphysical implications to imply that *things* are empty of own being, as Nishida, Nishitani, and Abe do. However, since God is not a thing among other things, a Buddhist needn't follow them in thinking that God is a thing among other things that is empty of being, too. In other words, it is possible for a Buddhist to take their *sunyata* experiences as revealing to them the far side of God who is not a thing and yet is also personal. Thus, it is *possible* for a Buddhist who accepts the fundamental metaphysical thesis of Buddhism, that all things are empty of being, to also accept the thesis that ultimate reality has both personal and suprapersonal aspects. This makes it possible for a Buddhist to accept Classical Theism, too.

Conclusion

The goal of this project has been simple. We aimed to show that a Buddhist can also be a Classical Theist. The most controversial part of establishing our thesis related to showing how the metaphysical frameworks of Classical Theism and Mere Buddhism are compatible. We took this challenge up first. Roughly, we argued that the philosophical theses of impermanence and interdependence only apply to "things," and since God, the immutable and absolutely independent ground of all reality, is not a thing, the core theses of Buddhism and Classical Theism are compatible. We engaged an objection that we shouldn't restrict the Buddhist theses to simply "all things" but rather to Being simpliciter. Utilizing primary sources, in the spirit of the Buddha, we argued that we didn't have to subject ourselves to heavy metaphysical doctrines beyond necessity.

In Chapters Two and Three, we engaged objections to Classical Theism. In Chapter Two we looked at objections from within the Buddhist context and in Chapter Three we engaged objections from the contemporary analytic literature, including the objection from omnisubjectivity, the problem of evil, and the threat of modal collapse.

In Chapters Four and Five, we synthesized ethical and soteriological systems. With respect to synthesizing ethical systems, we discussed how most Buddhist philosophers argue that there isn't one specific metaethical system that is endorsed in the Buddhist tradition. Rather, there seem to be deontological, virtue centered, and consequentialist components in the Buddhist tradition. Classical Theists, on the other hand, generally affirm at least some form of divine command theory.

We showed how divine command theory is compatible with both virtue-centered approaches and consequentialist accounts. We also argued that the Buddhist could consistently believe that God, wanting His creation to be enlightened, gives His creatures commands to encourage them to become virtuous, with the end of course enabling right realization. With respect to synthesizing soteriological systems, we surveyed the three Abrahamic traditions (Judaism, Christianity, and Islam) and showed how each endorses the view that there will be a resurrection of the just and the unjust. Those who follow the correct path will spend an eternity with God and those who fail to do so will end up in hell. This contrasts with the Buddhist tradition which emphasizes enlightenment. Specifically, the end goal is to escape suffering through the right realization that all things are impermanent and interdependent. We then argued, in effect, that the God of Classical Theism, too, could want His creatures to escape suffering in a similar way, which shows there to be overlap between the Buddhist and Christian conceptions of salvation.

Finally, in Chapters Six and Seven, we argued that we needn't look at Buddhist religious experience and theistic religious experience as experiences that are in fundamental tension or conflict. We argued, *contra* Hick, that religious experiences grounded in both traditions can be seen as mapping veridically onto reality. Specifically, we argued that characteristic Buddhist religious experiences could map onto the "far side" of God and that typical theistic religious experiences could map onto the "near side" of God. We then argued that it is possible for both Christians and Buddhists to accept the view that both of these religious experiences correspond to two different but consistent aspects of Being.

Having stated all this, we take it that we have shown one way in which Buddhism and Classical Theism can be synthesized. We hope that philosophers and theologians from all traditions will continue to explore and further explicate these issues from their respective creedal traditions. While this work has primarily been concerned with Classical Theism simpliciter, nonetheless—especially toward the end—we briefly discussed Christian doctrines as they relate to Buddhism. Specifically, we look forward to Catholic theologians continuing the project started here and exploring whether or not one can be both Catholic and Buddhist.

Notes

Introduction

1   Paul Williams, *The Unexpected Way* (Edinburgh: T & T Clark, 2002), 28.

2   Erik Baldwin and Tyler Dalton McNabb, *Plantingian Religious Epistemology and World Religions: Prospects and Problems* (Lanham, MD: Lexington Books, 2018).

3   Ibid., 179–81.

4   David Burton, *Buddhism: A Contemporary Philosophical Investigation* (Basingstoke: Taylor & Francis Ltd, 2017), 179.

5   Ibid., 180.

6   McDaniel, Jay, "Double Religious Belonging: A Process Approach," *Buddhist-Christian Studies* 23 (2003), 67.

7   Ibid., 76

8   Habito, Ruben L. F., "Buddhist? Christian? Both? Neither?," *Buddhist-Christian Studies*, 23 (2003), 52–3.

9   Ibid., 53

10 Fredericks, James L., "Review of Healing Breath: Zen for Christians and Buddhists in a Wounded World," *Buddhist-Christian Studies* 29 (2009), 153–5, 154.

11 Cornille, Catherine, "Double Religious Belonging: Aspects and Questions," *Buddhist-Christian Studies* 23 (2003), 45.

12 Ibid., 46.

13 See R. T. Mullins, *God and Emotions* (Cambridge: Cambridge University Press, 2020).

14 Aristotle, *Physics*, Book VII, 1, *The Complete Works of Aristotle: Volume One*, ed. Jonathan Barnes (Princeton: Princeton University Press, 1984), 407.

15 Edward Feser, *Scholastic Metaphysics: A Contemporary Introduction* (Neunkirchen-Seelscheid: Editiones-Scholasticae, 2014), 119.

16 The example used here is for the most part, is from Edward Feser's example in his *Thomas Aquinas: A Beginners Guide* (London: Oneworld Publications, 2009), 70.

17 For a thorough explication of this line of argument, see Edward Feser, *Five Proofs of the Existence of God* (San Francisco: Ignatius Press, 2017), Chapter 1.

18 Isaac Newton, *The Mathematical Principles of Natural Philosophy*, trans. Andrew Motte (New York: Daniel Adee, 1846), 83.

19 For more on this line of argument, Edward Feser, "Motion in Aristotle, Newton, and Einstein," in *Aristotle on Method and Metaphysics*, ed. Edward Feser (London: Palgrave Macmillan, 2013).

20 Edward Feser, *Aquinas: A Beginner's Guide* (Oxford: One World Publications, 2009), 78.

21 Graham Oppy, "On stage one of Feser's Aristotelian Proof," *Religious Studies*, published online October 30, 2019, forthcoming in print.

22 Ibid.

23 *Capturing Christianity*, "Are There Any Good Arguments for the Existence of God? Ed Feser v. Graham Oppy," www.youtube.com/watch?v=m-80lQOlNOs, accessed December 30, 2020.

24 Ibid.

25 A summary of Oppy's objections and a response to Oppy is further developed in Tyler Dalton McNabb and Michael DeVito, "Has Oppy Done away with the Aristotelian Proof?" *Heythrop Journal* 61, no. 5 (2020), 723–31.

Chapter 1

1 C. S. Lewis, *Mere Christianity* (New York: HarperCollins, 2017).

2 Jay Garfield, *Engaging Buddhism: Why It Matters to Philosophy* (Oxford: Oxford University Press, 2014), 2.

3 Ibid., 23.

4 David Burton, *Emptiness Appraised: A Critical Study of Nāgārjuna's Philosophy* (London: Routledge Press, 2015), 36.

5   Jan Westerhoff, *Nāgārjuna's Madhyamaka: A Philosophical Introduction*
    (New York: Oxford University Press, 2010), 26.

6   In addition to the doctrine of origination, Jan Westerhoff argues
    that there is another important dependence thesis that is affirmed in
    Buddhist traditions. Westerhoff argues that there is an idea of notional
    dependence, defined as follows: Objects falling under the property F
    are notionally dependent on objects falling under the property G iff
    necessarily, if some object x falls under F there will be a distinct object
    y falling under G. The idea is related to how Northern England in some
    sense depends on the Southern part of England. While technically
    something could happen to the Southern part of England without
    anything happening to Northern England (thus showing that Northern
    England isn't existentially dependent on Southern England), there is still
    a sense in which the concept of Northern England depends on Southern
    England. For the purpose of this book, it won't be important to explicate
    notional dependence in detail. As the reader will soon see, our argument
    for why a Mere Buddhist can endorse the doctrine of origination
    while accepting theism will be all encompassing such that it will cover
    notional dependence. See Westerhoff, *Nāgārjuna's Madhyamaka*, 26.

7   Garfield, *Engaging Buddhism*, 27.

8   Ibid., 33.

9   Ibid., 33.

10 Ibid., 42.

11 There are three approaches to understanding Nāgārjuna. First, there
    is the view that his work was a refutation of all knowledge. A second
    approach argues that Nāgārjuna's work argued against conceptual
    knowledge. The third approach however, argues that Nāgārjuna argued
    against the view that entities have intrinsic nature. This is the view that
    I am using here. See Burton, *Emptiness Appraised*, 2.

12 Westerhoff, *Nāgārjuna's Madhyamaka*, 19.

13 Garfield, *Engaging Buddhism*, 24.

14 Ibid., 62.

15 Tim Pawl, "Immutability," *Internet Encyclopedia of Philosophy*, https://
    www.iep.utm.edu/div-immu/.

16 William Vallicella, "Divine Simplicity," *Internet Encyclopedia of Philosophy*, Plato.Standford.edu/entries/divine-simplicity.

17 Alvin Plantinga, *Does God Have a Nature?* (Milwaukee: Marquette University Press, 1980), 47.

18 John Lamont, "Aquinas on Divine Simplicity," *The Monist* 80, no. 4 (1997), 529.

19 Ibid.

20 Ibid.

21 Etienne Gilson, *The Christian Philosophy of St. Thomas Aquinas* (Notre Dame: Notre Dame University Press, 1956), 107.

22 Ibid., 29, 30, 32.

23 Lamont, "Aquinas on Divine Simplicity," 530.

24 Brian Davies, "Is God a Moral Agent," in *Whose God? Which Tradition?* ed. D. Z. Phillips (Aldershot: Ashgate, 2009), 111.

25 Though it is important to note that Garfield seems to also use the word "entity" and even sometimes "thing" as well.

26 We are aware that some endorse what is called the Umbrella thesis, which states that all that exists falls under the category of object. Thus, an advocate of the Umbrella thesis might think that the words used by Garfield, Westerhoff, and Burton, are not restrictive. In accord with Classical Theism, we deny that God falls into this category and thus deny the Umbrella thesis. This is because God is not an object, and it isn't possible to include God in a category alongside other existent objects. On our view, the terms used above are restrictive in some sense. For more on the umbrella thesis, see, Bradley Rettler and Andrew Bailey, "Object," *Stanford Encyclopedia of Philosophy*, plato.stanford.edu/entries/object, accessed December 30, 2020.

27 David Bentley Hart seemingly endorses referring to God as a no-thing in *Experience of God: Being, Consciousness, Bliss* (New Haven: Yale University Press, 2014), 107.

28 See Stephan J. Laumakis, *An Introduction to Buddhist Philosophy* (Cambridge: Cambridge University Press, 2008): 147 and Jan Westerhoff, "Metaphysical Issues in Indian Buddhist Thought," in

A Companion to Buddhist Philosophy, ed. Steven M. Emmanuel
(Hoboken, NJ: Wiley-Blackwell, 2013), 138–9.

29   For instance, Descartes writes, "It will be impossible for anything to
obscure the clarity of this proof, if we attend to the nature of time
or of the duration of things. For the nature of time is such that its
parts are not mutually dependent, and never coexist. Thus, from
the fact that we now exist, it does not follow that we shall exist a
moment from now, unless there is some cause—the same cause
which originally produced us—which continually reproduces us,
as it were, that is to say, which keeps us in existence. For we easily
understand that there is no power in us enabling us to keep ourselves
in existence. We also understand that he who has so great a power
that he can keep us in existence, although we are distinct from him,
must be all the more able to keep himself in existence; or rather, he
requires no other being to keep him in existence, and hence, in short,
is God." ("*Principles of Philosophy*," in *The Philosophical Writings
of Descartes*, eds. John Cottingham, Robert Stoothoff, and Dugald
Murdoch (Cambridge: Cambridge University Press, 1985), 200).
And, according to Edwards, the cause of presently existing created
substance "can't be the antecedent existence of the same substance.
For instance, the existence of the body of the moon at this present
moment can't be the effect of its existence at the last foregoing
moment. For not only was what existed the last moment, no active
cause, but wholly a passive thing; but this also is to be considered,
that no cause can produce effects in a time and place on which itself is
not." "'Tis plain, nothing can exert itself, or operate, when and where
it is not existing. But the moon's past existence was neither where nor
when its present existence is." (*Original Sin*, in *The Works of Jonathan
Edwards*, vol. 3, ed. Clyde Holbrook (New Haven: Yale University
Press, 1970), 400).

30   David Vander Laan, "Creation and Conservation," *The Stanford
Encyclopedia of Philosophy* (Winter 2017 Edition), ed. Edward N.
Zalta, https://plato.stanford.edu/archives/win2017/entries/creation-
conservation/.

31   Brian Davies, "Letter from America," *New Black Friars,* vol. 84 (2007), 373.

32   Jonathan Edwards, *Original Sin*, in *The Works of Jonathan Edwards* Vl
     3, ed. Clyde Holbrook (New Haven: Yale University Press, 1970), 402.

33   Ibid., 404.

34   Ibid. For more on Edwards's view, see Jasper William Reid, "The
     Metaphysics of Jonathan Edwards and David Hume," *Hume Studies* 32
     (2006), 53–82.

35   See Gilbert Ryle, *The Concept of Mind* (Chicago: University of Chicago
     Press, 1949), 16–7.

36   K. T. S. Sarao, "Vasubandhu," *Internet Encyclopedia of Philosophy*,
     https://www.iep.utm.edu/vasubandhu/.

37   Mark Siderits, *Buddhism as Philosophy: An Introduction* (Aldershot:
     Ashgate, 2007), 172–3.

38   Masao Abe, "Sunyata as Formless Form," in *Zen and Comparative Studies*,
     ed. Steven Heine (Honolulu: University of Hawai'i Press, 1997), 139.

39   Ibid., 141.

40   Ibid.

41   Erik Baldwin, *Fully Informed Reasonable Disagreement and Tradition
     Based Perspectivalism*, Studies in Philosophical Theology. vol. 56
     (Leuven: Peeters Publishing, 2016), 99–100.

42   Masoa Abe, "Zen, Buddhism, and Western Thought," in *Zen and
     Western Thought* (Honolulu: University of Hawai'i Press, 1989), 94.

43   *The Shorter Exhortation to Malunkya Cula Malunkyovada Sutta*
     (MN 63), www.dhammatalks.org/suttas/MN/MN63.html, accessed
     December 30, 2020.

44   Ibid.

45   See *Dīgha-nikāya*, II, 55 and *Saṃyutta-nikāya*, II, 92 (12, 60).

46   We want to thank Rhett Gale for posing this objection.

47   Herbert McGabe, *God Matters* (London: Continuum, 2005), 6.

Chapter 2

1   See DN 11 of *Dīgha Nikāya*.

2   Roger Jackson, "Dharmakirti's Refutation of Theism," *Philosophy East
    and West* 36, no. 4 (1986), 320.

3 Burton points out "And yet, there is a long tradition of Buddhist critiques of God, usually aimed at concepts of the divine that occur in the varieties of Hinduism." See David Burton, *Buddhism: A Contemporary Philosophical Investigation* (New York: Routledge, 2017), 97.

4 Ernst Steinkellner, "Hindu Doctrines of Creation and Their Buddhist Critiques," in *Buddhism, Christianity and the Question of Creation: Karmic or Divine?*, ed. Perry Schmidt-Leukel (New York: Routledge, 2016), 31.

5 *Dharmakirti's Hetubindu* 4, 6f, as translated in Yoshimizu, 234, cited in Steinkellner, "Hindu Doctrines of Creation and Their Buddhist Critiques," 27.

6 Top of Form Eleonore Stump, *The God of the Bible and the God of the Philosophers* (Milwaukee: Marquette University Press, 2016), 28. Bottom of Form.

7 Ibid.

8 Ibid., 21.

9 Ibid., 37.

10 Ibid., 59–61.

11 Ibid., 57.

12 Burton, *Buddhism*, 97.

13 Descartes to Hyperaspistes, Aug. 1641, *The Philosophical Writings of Descartes*, vol. 3, trans. John Cottingham, Robert Stoothoff, Dugald Murdoch, and Anthony Kenny (Cambridge: Cambridge University Press, 1984).

14 Steinkellner, "Hindu Doctrines of Creation and Their Buddhist Critiques," 25.

15 See Alvin Plantinga, *God, Freedom, and Evil Plantinga* (Grand Rapids: William B. Eerdmans, 1977).

16 Here, we are using Michael Bergmann's argument found in "Common Sense Skeptical Theism," in *Science, Religion, and Metaphysics: New Essays on the Philosophy of Alvin Plantinga*, eds. K. Clark and M. Rea (Oxford: Oxford University Press, 2012), with Perry Hendrick's modifications found in Perry Hendricks, "Skeptical Theism Unscathed: Why Skeptical Objections to Skeptical Theism Fail," *Pacific Philosophical Quarterly* 101, no. 1, 43–73.

17 On our view, we can know what God would do in some situations. For example, if S has Scriptural support for believing that God wouldn't allow E in some instance, then S is in the position to make a judgment call about what God would or wouldn't do.

18 This example is used in Tyler Dalton McNabb, "Pestilent Pope or a Pestilent Church?: Judaism, Catholicism, and Skeptical Theism," *Heythrop Journal* (2020): 61/4: 671–676, https://doi.org/10.1111/heyj.13571

19 Isiah 55:8–9, NIV Translation.

20 1 Corinthians 1:25, NIV Translation.

21 Sahih Translation.

22 Ibid.

23 Hud Hudson, "The Father of Lies?" in *Oxford Studies in Philosophy of Religion*, vol. 5, ed. Jonathon L. Kvanvig (Oxford: Oxford University Press, 2014), 163.

24 Wielenberg's arguments are somewhat inspired by the Biblical text. For example, Wielenberg states that, God knew both (i) His command to Abraham would cause Abraham to believe (reasonably) that Abraham was going to sacrifice Isaac and (ii) Abraham was not going to sacrifice Isaac. We grant Hubert Martin's assessment that "in testing Abraham, God ... deceives him." See, Erik J. Wielenberg, "Divine Deception," in *Skeptical Theism: New Essays*, eds. Trent Dougherty and Justin P. McBrayer (Oxford: Oxford University Press, 2014), 242.

25 Erik Wielenberg, "Skeptical Theism and Divine Lies," *Religious Studies* 46 (2010), 513.

26 Kenneth Boyce, "Proper Functionalism," *Internet Encyclopedia of Philosophy*, https://www.iep.utm.edu/prop-fun/.

27 See, for instance, Alvin Plantinga, *God and Other Minds: A Study of the Rational Justification of Belief in God* (Ithaca, NY: Cornell University Press, 1967).

28 Erik Baldwin and Tyler Dalton McNabb, *Plantingian Religious Epistemology and World Religions* (Lanham: Lexington Books, 2018), 271.

29 Hendricks, "Skeptical Theism Unscathed: Why Skeptical Objections to Skeptical Theism Fail," 55.
30 Ibid.

Chapter 3

1   R. T. Mullins briefly discusses this in *God and Emotions* (Cambridge: Cambridge University Press, 2020).
2   For this style of argument, see Norman Kretzmann, "Omniscience and Immutability," *The Journal of Philosophy* 63, no. 14 (1966), 409–21.
3   Ibid., 410.
4   Thomas Sullivan, "Omniscience, Immutability, and the Divine Mode of Knowing," *Faith and Philosophy* 8, no. 1 (1991), 25–6.
5   Sullivan also takes it that simplicity plays an important role in discussing how God knows facts. See Ibid., 30.
6   Tim Pawl seems to have this worry in his Tim Pawl, "Immutability," *Internet Encyclopedia of Philosophy*, https://www.iep.utm.edu/div-immu/.
7   For more on this point, see Michael Rea, *The Hiddenness of God* (Oxford: Oxford University Press, 2018).
8   Frank Jackson, "Epiphenomenal Qualia," *Philosophical Quarterly* 32 (1982), 130.
9   Mullins, *God and Emotions*, 30.
10 Ibid., 4.
11 Ibid., 32.
12 Thomas Nagel, "What Is It Like to Be a Bat?," *Philosophical Review* 83 (1974), 435–50.
13 This is actually how Molinia grounded God's middle knowledge. See Kirk McGregor, *Luis de Molina: The Life and Theology of the Founder of Middle Knowledge* (Grand Rapids: Zondervan Publishing, 2018).
14 Mullins, *God and Emotions*, 42.
15 Ibid., 46.
16 Ibid., 48.

17 Ibid., 49.

18 Some of the following section was published in, Tyler Dalton McNabb and Michael DeVito, "Has Oppy Done away with the Aristotelian Proof?" *Heythrop Journal* 61, no. 5 (2020), 723–1.

19 William Abraham, *Divine Agency and Divine Action: Exploring and Evaluating the Debate* (New York: Oxford University Press, 2018), 179–80.

20 W. Matthews Grant, "Can a Libertarian Hold That Our Free Actions Are Caused by God?" *Faith and Philosophy* 27, no. 1 (2010), 22.

21 Ibid., 25.

22 Ibid., 25. Cf. Robert Kane, *A Contemporary Introduction to Free Will* (New York: Oxford University Press, 2005), 5–6.

23 Grant, "Can a Libertarian Hold That Our Free Actions Are Caused by God?", 26.

24 Ibid., 31.

25 Ibid.

26 Ibid.; Timothy O'Connor, "Simplicity and Creation," *Faith and Philosophy* 16, no. 3 (1999), 408.

27 R. T. Mullins, *The End of the Timeless God* (New York: Oxford University Press, 2016), 138.

28 Christopher Tomaszewski, "Collapsing the Modal Collapse Argument: On an Invalid Argument against Divine Simplicity," *Analysis* 79 (2019), 277.

29 Ibid., 28.

30 See, for example, Edward Feser's critique of Mullins, Edward Feser, "A Further Reply to Mullins on Divine Simplicity," edwardfeser.blogspot.com/2019/08/a-further-reply-to-mullins-on-divine.html, accessed December 30, 2020.

31 See James Anderson, *Paradox in Christian Theology: An Analysis of Its Presence, Character, and Epistemic Status* (London: Paternoster Press, 2007).

32 James Anderson, "In Defence of Mystery: A Reply to Dale Tuggy," *Religious Studies* 41, no. 2 (2005), 149.

33 Kenneth Boyce, "Proper Functionalism," *Internet Encyclopedia of Philosophy*, https://www.iep.utm.edu/prop-fun/.

34 Paul Tillich, *Systematic Theology*, 3 vols (Chicago: University of Chicago Press, 1951–63), 205.

35 Thomas Aquinas, *Summa Theologiae* Ia. A. 12, art. 1, obj. 3. In Robert R. N. Ross, "The Non-Existence of God: Tillich, Aquinas, and the Pseudo-Dionysius," *The Harvard Theological Review* 68, no. 2 (1975), 142.

Chapter 4

1 Maria Heim, *Buddhist Ethics* (Cambridge: Cambridge University Press, 2019), 2.

2 Ibid.

3 Ibid., 9.

4 Jay Garfield, *Engaging Buddhism: Why It Matters to Philosophy* (Oxford: Oxford University Press, 2015), 285.

5 Ibid., 280.

6 Ibid.

7 Heim, *Buddhist Ethics*, 38.

8 Garfield, *Engaging Buddhism*, 299.

9 Ibid., 286.

10 There are some today who want to downplay the role of karma in Buddhist ethics. However, the separation between Karma and ethics isn't justified. Heim makes this point well when she states that, "Although some modern Buddhist figures (such as Stephen Batchelor) have questioned or downplayed samsara in their formulations of Buddhism, samsara and karma are foundational for the Buddha, Buddhaghosa, and Santideva, and it will be difficult to make sense of their moral and soteriological paths without them." See Heim, *Buddhist Ethics*, 9.

11 Garfield, *Engaging Buddhism*, 284.

12 David Burton, *Buddhism: A Contemporary Philosophical Investigation* (London: Routledge Taylor & Francis Group, 2017), 38.

13 Even someone like Richard Swinburne, who argues that most moral facts are necessary moral truths, thinks that at least some of our obligations are grounded in God's commands. He argues that "the existence and actions of God make a great difference to what these [necessary moral truths] are." (Richard Swinburne, "What Difference Does God Make to Morality?" in *Is Goodness Without God Good Enough?: A Debate on Faith, Secularism, and Ethics*, eds. Robert K. Garcia and Nathan L. King (Lanham: Rowman and Littlefield, 2009), 155.

14 For defences of divine command theory, see Tyler Dalton McNabb, "Wiley Coyote and the Craggy Rocks Below: The Perils of Godless Ethics," *Philosophia Christi* 20, no. 2 (2018), 339–46; David Baggett and Jerry L. Walls, *God and Cosmos: Moral Truth and Human Meaning* (Oxford: Oxford University Press, 2016); William Lane Craig, *Reasonable Faith: Christian Truth and Apologetics* (Wheaton: Crossway Books), 2009.

15 See Plato's *The Euthyphro in Plato*; Benjamin Jowett, and J. D. Kaplan, *Dialogues of Plato* (New York: Pocket Books, 2001).

16 See, for instance, Joseph J. Kotva, Jr., *The Christian Case for Virtue Ethics* (Plymouth: Georgetown University Press, 1996) and David McPherson, *Virtue and Meaning: A Neo-Aristotelian Perspective* (Cambridge: Cambridge University Press, 2020). For virtue inspired accounts, see David S. Oderberg, *Moral Theory: A Non-Consequentialist Approach* (Hoboken, NJ: Wiley-Blackwell, 2000) and the works of Alasdair MacIntyre, a good summary of which is David Solomon, "MacIntyre and Contemporary Moral Philosophy," in *Alasdair MacIntyre*, ed. Mark C. Murphy (Cambridge: Cambridge University Press, 2003), 114–151.

17 William Paley, *The Principles of Moral and Political Philosophy* (Indianapolis: Liberty Fund, 2002).

18 See Ancius Boethius, *The Consolation of Philosophy* (Westminster: Penguin Classics, 1999).

19 There is some ambiguity with respect to if happiness is achieved by knowing God or acting virtuous. As John Marenbon points out,

"Philosophy seems to speak as if, merely by knowing that God is perfect happiness, Boethius himself will be rendered happy, although in the next section it seems that it is by acting well that a person can attain the good." John Marenbon, "Ancius Manlius Severinus Boethius," *Stanford Encyclopedia of Philosophy*, https://plato.stanford.edu/entries/boethius.

20 John Stuart Mill, *Utilitarianism*, ed. Roger Crisp (Oxford: Oxford University Press, 2004), 56, 64.

21 Ibid., 82–4, 86.

22 RSV Exodus 20:2–18.

23 Damien Keown, *Buddhist Ethics: A Very Short Introduction* (Oxford, UK: Oxford University Press, 2005), 7.

24 RSV Exodus 20:2–18.

25 In Peter Harvey, *An Introduction to Buddhist Ethics* (Cambridge, UK: Cambridge University Press, 2000), 289.

26 Ibid., 71.

27 Burton, *Buddhism*, 56.

Chapter 5

1 Those who adhere to what will later be referred to as Judaism, affirm the following:

1. I believe with perfect faith that the Creator, blessed be his name, is the Author and Guide of everything that has been created, and that he alone has made, does make, and will make all things.

2. I believe with perfect faith that the Creator, blessed be his name, is a Unity, and that there is no unity in any manner like unto his, and that he alone is our God, who was, is, and will be.

3. I believe with perfect faith that the Creator, blessed be his name, is not a body, and that he is free from all the accidents of matter, and that he has not any form whatsoever.

4. I believe with perfect faith that the Creator, blessed be his name, is the first and the last.

5. I believe with perfect faith that to the Creator, blessed be his name, and to him alone, it is right to pray, and that it is not right to pray to any being besides him.
6. I believe with perfect faith that all the words of the prophets are true.
7. I believe with perfect faith that the prophecy of Moses our teacher, peace be unto him, was true, and that he was the chief of the prophets, both of those that preceded and of those that followed him.
8. I believe with perfect faith that the whole Law, now in our possession, is the same that was given to Moses our teacher, peace be unto him.
9. I believe with perfect faith that this Law will not be changed, and that there will never be any other law from the Creator, blessed be his name.
10. I believe with perfect faith that the Creator, blessed be his name, knows every good deed of the children of men, and all their thoughts, as it is said, It is he that fashioneth the hearts of them all, that giveth to all their deeds.
11. I believe with perfect faith that the Creator, blessed be his name, rewards those that keep his commandments, and punished those that transgress them.
12. I believe with perfect faith in the coming Messiah, and, though he may tarry, I will wait daily for his coming.
13. I believe with prefect faith that there will be a resurrection of the dead at the time when it shall please the Creator, blessed be his name, and exalted be the remembrance of him for ever and ever!

See Moses Maimonides, "Thirteen Principles of the Faith," in *The Standard Prayer Book*, trans. Simeon Singer (New York: Bloch Publishing Company, 1915), 107–9.

2 This is taken from, Chabad.Org, "The 7 Noahide Laws: Universal Morality," www.chabad.org/library/article_cdo/aid/62221/jewish/The-7-Noahide-Laws-Universal-Morality, accessed December 30, 2020.

3   For a discussion on this, see Samuel Lebens, *The Principles of Judaism* (Oxford: Oxford University Press, 2020), 236.

4   See United States Conferences of Catholic Bishops, What We Believe, www.usccb.org/beliefs-and-teachings/what-we-believe, accessed December 30, 2020.

5   *The Catechism of the Catholic Church*, second edition, section 847.

6   *Karl Rahner in Dialogue: Conversations and Interviews, 1965–82*, eds. Paul Imhof and Hubert Biallowons, trans. Harvey D. Egan (New York: Crossroad, 1986), 135.

7   See, for instance, Clark H. Pinnock, *A Wideness in God's Mercy: The Finality of Jesus Christ in a World of Religions* (Grand Rapids, MI: Zondervan, 1992).

8   See Hans Urs von Balthasar, *Dare We Hope "That All Men Be Saved"?* (San Francisco: Ignatius Press, 2014) and Thomas Talbott, *The Inescapable Love of God: Second Edition* (Eugene, OR: Wipf and Stock Publishers, 2014).

9   For more on *The Five Pillars*, see Mauluna Muhammad Ali, *The Religion of Islam: A Comprehensive Discussion of the Sources, Principles, and Practices of Islam* (Columbus: Amaddiyya Anjuman Isha'at Islam, 1990), 99–101, 263–442 and Saeed Abdullah, *Islamic Thought: An Introduction* (Abingdon, UK: Routledge, 2006), 3.

10   The text is taken from an influential Sunni Creed, *Abū Ja'far al-Ṭaḥāwī, Al-Aqidah al-Tahawiyya*, translated by Abu Amina Elias, https://abuaminaelias.com/aqeedah-tahawiyyah/, accessed December 30, 2020.

11   Walpola Rahula, *What the Buddha Taught* (New York: Grove Press, 1959), 17.

12   Adapted from C. S. Prebish and D. Keown, *Introducing Buddhism* (New York and London: Routledge, 2006), 52–4.

13   In Bary William Theodore de, ed., *The Buddhist Tradition in India, China and Japan* (New York: Vintage Books, 1972), 29.

14   Ibid., 29.

15   Rudi Maire, "Salvation in Buddhism," *Journal of Adventist Mission Studies* 10, no. 1 (2014), 26.

16 Jay Garfield, *Engaging Buddhism: Why It Matters to Philosophy* (Oxford: Oxford University Press, 2014), 2.

17 Ibid.

Chapter 6

1 John Hick, *An Interpretation of Religion* (New Haven: Yale University Press, 1989), 241–2.

2 Thomas Kelly, "Peer Disagreement and High Level Evidence," in *Disagreement*, eds. Richard Feldman and Ted Warfield (New York: Oxford University Press, 2010), 112.

3 Joseph Kim, *Reformed Epistemology and the Problem of Religious Diversity: Proper Function, Epistemic Disagreement, and Christian Exclusivism* (Cambridge: James Clarke, 2012), 49–50.

4 Alvin Plantinga articulates this line of reasoning in John Hick, *Dialogues in the Philosophy of Religion* (London: Palgrave Macmillan, 2010), 54–5.

5 Tyler Dalton McNabb, *Religious Epistemology* (Cambridge: Cambridge University Press, 2018), 31.

6 Kim, *Reformed Epistemology and the Problem of Religious Diversity*, 56.

7 The following facts and reasoning expressed related to the resurrection can be found in William Lane Craig, *The Son Rises* (Eugene: Wipf Stock Publishers, 2000).

8 Josephus, *Antiquities*, Book 18.

9 Tacitus, *Annals* book 15, Chapter 44.

10 Craig, *The Son Rises*, 53.

11 Ibid., 60.

12 Ibid., 91–107.

13 See Sean McDowell, *The Fate of the Apostles: Examining the Martyrdom Accounts of the Closest Followers of Jesus* (London: Routledge, 2016).

14 See Gary Habermas's personal correspondence with psychologist Gary Sibey and Michael Licona's personal correspondence with psychologist Frank Larøi in Michael Licona, *The Historicity of the Resurrection of*

Jesus: Historiographical Considerations in the Light of Recent Debates (Downers Grove: Intervarsity Press, 2013), 484–5.

15 John Hick, *The Metaphor of God Incarnate: Christology in a Pluralistic Age* (Louisville, KY: Westminster John Knox Press, 2006), 24.

16 Ibid., 16.

17 Brant James Pitre, *The Case for Jesus: The Biblical and Historical Evidence for Christ* (New York: Penguin Random House, 2016), 14–6.

18 Richard Bauckham makes this argument in *Jesus and the Eyewitnesses: The Gospels as Eyewitness Testimony* (Grand Rapids: Eerdmans Publishing Company, 2006), 52.

19 Ibid.

20 Zain Ali, "An Evidential Argument for Islamic Theism," *European Journal for Philosophy of Religion* 10, no. 4 (2018), 55–78.

21 Much of what follows is taken from Tyler Dalton McNabb and Joseph Blado, "Mary and Fátima: A Modest C-Inductive Argument for Catholicism," *Perichoresis* 18, no. 5 (2020), 55–65.

22 See Stanley Jaki's discussion of Catholicism pre-1917 in *God and the Sun at Fatima* (Royal Oak, MI: Real View Books, 1999).

23 Roy Abraham Varghese, *God-Sent: A History of the Accredited Apparitions of Mary* (New York: Crossroad Pub. Co, 2011), 109.

24 Ibid., 109–110.

25 Ibid., 110.

26 For more information on this, see Jeffery S. Bennett, *When the Sun Danced: Myth, Miracles, and Modernity in Early Twentieth-Century Portugal* (Charlottesville: University of Virginia Press, 2012).

27 Varghese, *God-Sent*, 111.

28 For a lengthy account, see Bennett, *When the Sun Danced.*

29 Ibid.

30 See Jaki, *God and the Sun at Fatima*, 170–1; J. M. Haffert, *Meet the Witnesses* (Washington, NJ: World Apostolate of Fátima, 1988).

31 Jaki, *God and the Sun at Fatima*, 303.

32 Monique Hope-Ross, Stephen Travers, and David Mooney, "Solar retinopathy following religious rituals," *British Journal of Opthalmology*, 72 (1988), 931–4.

33　See Auguste Meesen, "Apparitions and Miracles of the Sun," *International Forum in Porto, "Science, Religion, and Conscience,"* October 23–25, 2003.

34　Hope-Ross, Travers, and Mooney, "Solar Retinopathy Following Religious Rituals," 933.

35　This is what seems to be implied in Mrs. da Silva's report of her two employees, Albano Barro's report, and Godinho's report in, Haffert, *Meet the Witnesses*.

36　Jaki, *God and the Sun at Fatima*, 348–9.

Chapter 7

1　A comparison between John's Buddhist religious experience and Paul's Christian religious experience was originally developed in Chapter 4 of Erik Baldwin, "Fully Informed Reasonable Disagreement and Tradition Based Perspectivalism," Dissertation, *Purdue*, (2012): accessible https://docs.lib.purdue.edu/dissertations/AAI3543354/; Chapter 4 of Erik Baldwin, *Reasonable Disagreement and Tradition Based Perspectivalism* (Leuven: Peeters Publisher, 2016). This comparison, however, was originally developed and employed for an altogether different purpose than the purpose of this chapter.

2　Robert Wilkinson, *Nishida and Western Philosophy* (Farnham: Ashgate, 2009), 9.

3　Ibid., 7–9. Wilkinson derives aspects of his analysis from D.T. Suzuki's *Essays in Zen Buddhism*, 1st and 2nd series (London: Luzac, 1927 and 1933).

4　For example, see L.F. Ruben Habito, "Buddhist? Christian? Both? Neither?," *Buddhist-Christian Studies*, no. 23 (2003) and "Being Buddhist, Being Christian: Being Both, Being Neither," in *Converging Ways?: Conversion and Belonging in Buddhism and Christianity*, ed. John D'Arcy May (Sankt Ottilien: EOS Klosterverlag, 2007), 165–80; Donald W Mitchell and O.S.B James Wiseman, eds., *The Gethsemani Encounter: A Dialogue on the Spiritual Life by Buddhist and Christian*

Monastics (New York: Continuum, 1997); John D'Arcy May, ed., *Converging Ways?: Conversion and Belonging in Buddhism and Christianity* (Sankt Ottilien: EOS Klosterverlag, 2007); and Robert Aitken and David Steindl-Rast, *The Ground We Share: Everyday Practice, Buddhist and Christian* (Liguori: Triumph Books, 1994).

5   On double religious belonging, see Catherine Cornille, "Double Religious Belonging: Aspects and Questions", *Buddhist-Christian Studies*, no. 23 (2003), 43–9, Habito (2003) and (2007), Paul F. Knitter, *Without Budda I Could Not Be a Christian* (Oxford: One World, 2009), and Jay McDaniel, "Double Religious Belonging: A Process Approach," *Buddhist-Christian Studies*, no. 23 (2003), 67–76.

6   This distinction is controversial, but we take it that it is both intelligible and philosophically defensible Nagarjuna offers the seminal defense of the view in his *Mulamadhyamakakarika*, or *Fundamental Treatise on the Middle Way*. For a contemporary translation with commentary, see Garfield (1995). Geshe Tashi Tsering provides a nice study of the distinction as it appears in various forms of Buddhism in his *Emptiness, The Foundations of Buddhist Thought*, vol. 5 (Somerville, MA: Wisdom Publications, Inc., 2018).

7   Masao Abe, "Emptiness," in *Zen and Comparative Studies*, ed. Steven Heine (Honolulu: University of Hawai'i Press, 1997), 51.

8   Ibid., 52.

9   William James, "A World of Pure Experience," *The Journal of Philosophy, Psychology and Scientific Methods* 1, no. 20 (1904), 533–43.

10   Krueger, Joel W., "The Varieties of Pure Experience: William James and Kitaro Nishida on Consciousness and Embodiment," *William James Studies* 1, no. 1 (2006), Jul. 2009. <http://williamjamesstudies.press. illinois.edu/1.1/krueger.html>.

11   See Kitaro Nishida, *An Inquiry Into the Good* (New Haven and London: Yale University Press, 1990): 3–10.

12   Ibid., 3–4. Italics are ours.

13   Nishida, *An Inquiry Into the Good*, 31.

14   The full passage reads, "There is no difference at all between Samsara and Nirvana! There is no difference at all between Nirvana and

Samsara! [They are both empty (*shunya*) of essence.]" See Nagarjuna, *Mulamadhyamaka-Karika*, (*The Fundamentals of the Middle Way*), ed. George Cronk, (1998), 167.

15 From *The Heart Sutra, with Commentary*, trans. R. Pine (Washington, DC: Shoemaker and Hoard Publishers, 2004), 2.

16 Donald W. Mitchell, *Spirituality and Emptiness* (Mahwah: Paulist Press, 1991), 23.

17 Wolfhart Pannenberg, "The Abe-Pannenberg Encounter, Afterword," in *Masao Abe: A Life of Zen Dialogue*, ed. D. W. Mitchell (Boston: Tutle Publishing, 1998), 208.

18 Clarence Edwin Rolt, *Dionysius the Areopagite: On the Divine Names and the Mystical Theology* (Grand Rapids: Christian Classics Ethereal Library, 1920), 51–2.

19 Ibid., 51–4.

20 *Summa Theologica*, Iᵃ q. 13 a. 2 co. Text taken from Thomas Aquinas, *Selected Philosophical Writings*, trans. and ed. Timothy McDermott (Oxford: Oxford University Press, 1993), 217–8.

21 This passage is from the *New American Standard Bible*.

22 David Brown, *The Divine Trinity* (La Salle: Open Court, 1985), 102–3.

23 While this model seems more theologically appropriate, we want to clarify that we are not intending the discussion here to be an endorsement of a kenotic Christology or Trinitarianism.

24 Ronald J. Feenstra, "Reconsidering Kenotic Christology," in *Trinity, Incarnation, and Atonement: Philosophical and Theological Essays*, eds. Ronald J. Feenstra and Cornelius Plantinga, Jr. (Indiana: University of Notre Dame Press, 1989), 130–1.

Works Cited

Abe, Masao. "Zen and Western Thought." *International Philosophical Quarterly* 10, no. 4 (1970): 501–41.

Abe, Masao. "Emptiness." In *Zen and Comparative Studies*, edited by Steven Heine. Honolulu: University of Hawai'i Press, 1997, 42–53.

Abe, Masao. "Sunyata as Formless Form." In *Zen and Comparative Studies*, edited by Steven Heine. Honolulu: University of Hawai'i Press, 1997, 139–48.

Abdullah, Saeed. *Islamic Thought: An Introduction*. Abingdon, UK: Routledge, 2006.

Abū Jaʿfar al-Ṭaḥāwī, Al-Aqidah al-Tahawiyya, translated by Abu Amina Elias, https://abuaminaelias.com/aqeedah-tahawiyyah/?fbclid=IwAR0NW 1yW8A49UjMyN8aggzv5-hjmI_u0caNS9zEUXsO5jfwNqDiHr0BYk1Y.

Aitken, Robert and David Steindl-Rast. *The Ground We Share: Everyday Practice, Buddhist and Christian*. Liguori: Triumph Books, 1994.

Aleman, Andre and Frank Laroi. *Hallucinations: The Science of Idiosyncratic Perception*. Washington, DC: American Psychological Association, 2008.

Ali, Mauluna Muhammad. *The Religion of Islam: A Comprehensive Discussion of the Sources, Principles, and Practices of Islam*. Columbus: Amaddiyya Anjuman Isha'at Islam, 1990.

Ali, Zain. "An Evidential Argument for Islamic Theism." *European Journal for Philosophy of Religion* 10, no. 4 (2018): 55–78.

Anderson, James. "In Defence of Mystery: A Reply to Dale Tuggy." *Religious Studies* 41, no. 2 (2005): 145–63.

Anderson, James. *Paradox in Christian Theology: An Analysis of Its Presence, Character, and Epistemic Status*. London: Paternoster Press, 2007.

Aquinas, Thomas. *Summa Theologica: Complete English Edition in Five Volumes*. Westminster: Christian Classics, 1981.

Aquinas, Thomas. *Aquinas: Selected Philosophical Writings*, translated by Timothy McDermott. Oxford: Oxford University Press, 1993.

Abraham, William. *Divine Agency and Divine Action: Exploring and Evaluating the Debate*. New York: Oxford University Press, 2018.

Baggett, David and Jerry L. Walls. *God and Cosmos: Moral Truth and Human Meaning*. Oxford: Oxford University Press, 2016.

Baldwin, Erik. *Fully Informed Reasonable Disagreement and Tradition Based Perspectivalism*. Studies in Philosophical Theology. vol. 56. Leuven: Peeters Publishing, 2016.

Baldwin, Erik and Tyler McNabb. *Plantingian Religious Epistemology and World Religions: Prospects and Problems*. Lanham: Lexington Books, 2018.

Bauckham, Richard. *Jesus and the Eyewitnesses: The Gospels as Eyewitness Testimony*. Grand Rapids: Eerdmans Publishing Company, 2017.

Bennett, Jeffery S. *When the Sun Danced: Myth, Miracles, and Modernity in Early Twentieth-Century Portugal*. Charlottesville: University of Virginia Press, 2012.

Boethius, Ancius. *The Consolation of Philosophy*. Westminster: Penguin Classics, 1999.

Brown, David. *The Divine Trinity*. La Salle: Open Court Publishing Company, 1985.

Burton, David. *Emptiness Appraised: A Critical Study of Nāgārjuna's Philosophy*. London: Routledge Press, 2015.

Boyce, Kenneth. "Proper Functionalism." *Internet Encyclopedia of Philosophy*, https://www.iep.utm.edu/prop-fun/

Chabad.org, The 7 Noahide Laws: Universal Morality, accessed April 22, 2020. https://www.chabad.org/library/article_cdo/aid/62221/jewish/the-7-noahide-laws-universal-morality.htm?gclid=cjwkcajw1v_0brakeiwalfkj5gi5usxpbhnci4vc0eud_pzlz7jluaivbfaka4inxzu_imomcbdjlbocy0kqavd_bwe.

Cornille, Catherine. "Double Religious Belonging: Aspects and Questions." *Buddhist-Christian Studies*, no. 23 (2003): 43–9.

Craig, William. *The Son Rises*. Eugene: Wipf Stock Publishers, 2000.

Craig, William. Lane *Reasonable Faith: Christian Truth and Apologetics*. Wheaton: Crossway Books, 2009.

Davies, Brian. "Is God a Moral Agent?" In *Whose God? Which Tradition?*, edited by D. Z. Phillips. Aldershot: Ashgate, 2009, 97–122.

Davies, Brian. "Letter from America." *New Black Friars* (2007): 998–9.

De Bary, William Theodore, ed. *The Buddhist Tradition in India, China and Japan*. New York: Vintage Books, 1972.

Descartes, Rene. *The Philosophical Writings of Descartes*, vol. 1, edited by John Cottingham, Robert Stoothoff, and Dugald Murdoch. Cambridge: Cambridge University Press, 1985.

Edwards, Jonathan. *Original Sin*, in *The Works of Jonathan Edwards*, vol. 3, edited by Clyde Holbrook. New Haven: Yale University Press, 1970.

Feenstra, Ronald J. "Reconsidering Kenotic Christology." In *Trinity, Incarnation, and Atonement: Philosophical and Theological Essays*, edited by Ronald J. Feenstra and Jr. Cornelius Plantinga. Notre Dame: University of Notre Dame Press, 1989.

Feser, Edward. "A Further Reply to Mullins on Divine Simplicity," accessed November 12, 2019, http://edwardfeser.blogspot.com/2019/08/a-further-reply-to-mullins-on-divine.html.

Garfield, Jay L. *Engaging Buddhism: Why It Matters to Philosophy*. Oxford: Oxford University Press, 2014.

Gilson, Etienne. *The Christian Philosophy of St. Thomas Aquinas*. Notre Dame: Notre Dame University Press, 1956.

Grant, W. Matthews. "Can a Libertarian Hold That Our Free Actions Are Caused by God?" *Faith and Philosophy* 27, no. 1 (2010): 22–44.

Habito, Ruben L.F. "Buddhist? Christian? Both? Neither?" *Buddhist-Christian Studies* 23, no. 23 (2003): 51–3.

Habito, Ruben L.F. "Being Buddhist, Being Christian: Being Both, Being Neither." In *Converging Ways?: Conversion and Belonging in Buddhism and Christianity*, edited by John D'Arcy May. Sankt Ottilien: EOS Klosterverlag, 2007, 165–80.

Haffert, J. M. *Meet the Witnesses*. Washington, DC: World Apostolate of Fátima, 1988.

Harvey, Peter. *An Introduction to Buddhist Ethics*. Cambridge: Cambridge University Press, 2000.

The Heart Sutra, with Commentary, translated by R. Pine. Washington, DC: Shoemaker and Hoard Publishers, 2004.

Heim, Maria. *Buddhist Ethics*. Cambridge: Cambridge University Press, 2019.

Heisig, James W. "East-West Dialogue: Sunyata and Kenosis." *Spirituality Today* 39 (1987): 358–83

Hendricks, Perry. "Skeptical Theism Unscathed: Why Skeptical Objections to Skeptical Theism Fail." *Pacific Philosophical Quarterly* 101, no. 1 (2020): 43–73.

Hick, John. *Dialogues in the Philosophy of Religion*. London: Palgrave Macmillan, 2010.

Hick, John. *The Metaphor of God Incarnate: Christology in a Pluralistic Age.* Louisville, KY: Westminster John Knox Press, 2006.

Hope-Ross, Monique, Stephen Travers, and David Mooney. "Solar Retinopathy Following Religious Rituals." *British Journal of Opthalmology* 72 (1988): 931–4.

Hudson, Hud. "The Father of Lies?" In *Oxford Studies in Philosophy of Religion, vol. 5*, edited by Jonathon L. Kvanvig. Oxford: Oxford University Press, 2014, 147–66.

Imhof, Paul and Hubert Biallowons. *Karl Rahner in Dialogue: Conversations and Interviews*, edited and translation by Harvey D. Egan. New York: Crossroad, 1986.

Ingram, Paul O. *The Process of Buddhist-Christian Dialogue*. Eugene: Cascade Books, 2009.

Jackson, Frank. "Epiphenomenal Qualia." *Philosophical Quarterly* 32 (1982): 127–36.

Jaki, Stanley. *God and the Sun at Fatima*. Royal Oak, MI: Real View Books, 1999.

James, William. "A World of Pure Experience." *The Journal of Philosophy, Psychology and Scientific Methods* 1, no. 20 (1904): 533–43.

Josephus, Flavius. *Antiquities of the Jews, in Complete Works of Josephus; the Wars of the Jews, against Apion*, edited by Samuel Donaldson. London: Forgotten Books, 2012.

Kane, Robert. *A Contemporary Introduction to Free Will*. New York: Oxford University Press, 2005.

Kelly, Thomas. "Peer Disagreement and Higher Order Evidence." In *Disagreement*, edited by Richard Feldman and Ted Warfield. Oxford, UK: Oxford University Press, 2008, 111–174.

Keown, Damien. *Buddhist Ethics: A Very Short Introduction*. Oxford, UK: Oxford University Press, 2005.

Kim, Joseph. *Reformed Epistemology and the Problem of Religious Diversity: Proper Function, Epistemic Disagreement, and Christian Exclusivism.* Eugene: Pickwick Publications, 2011.

Knitter, Paul F. *Without Buddha I Could Not Be a Christian.* Oxford: One World, 2009.

Kotva, Joseph J. Jr. *The Christian Case for Virtue Ethics.* Plymouth: Georgetown University Press, 1996.

Kretzmann, Norman. "Omniscience and Immutability." *The Journal of Philosophy* 63, no. 14 (1966): 409–21.

Krueger, Joel. "The Varieties of Pure Experience: William James and Kitaro Nishida on Consciousness and Embodiment." *William James Studies* 1, no. 1 (2009): 1–16.

Laumakis, Stephan J. *An Introduction to Buddhist Philosophy.* Cambridge, UK: Cambridge University Press, 2008.

Lamont, John. "Aquinas on Divine Simplicity." *The Monist* 80, no. 4 (1997): 521–38.

Lebens, Samuel. *The Principles of Judaism.* Oxford: Oxford University Press, 2020.

Lewis, C.S. *Mere Christianity.* New York: HarperCollins, 2017.

Licona, Michael. *The Historicity of the Resurrection of Jesus: Historiographical Considerations in the Light of Recent Debates.* Downers Grove: Intervarsity Press, 2013.

Maimonides, Moses. "Thirteen Principles of the Faith." In *The Standard Prayer Book*, translated by Simeon Singer. New York: Bloch Publishing Company, 1915, 107–109.

Maier, Rudi. "Salvation in Buddhism." *Journal of Adventist Mission Studies* 10, no. 1 (2014): 9–42.

Marenbon, John. "Ancius Manlius Severinus Boethius." *Stanford Encyclopedia of Philosophy*, https://plato.stanford.edu/entries/boethius.

McDaniel, Jay. "Double Religious Belonging: A Process Approach." *Buddhist-Christian Studies* 23, no. 23 (2003): 67–76.

McDowell, Sean. *The Fate of the Apostles: Examining the Martyrdom Accounts of the Closest Followers of Jesus.* London: Routledge, 2016.

McGregor, Kirk. *Luis De Molina: The Life and Theology of the Founder of Middle Knowledge.* Grand Rapids: Zondervan, 2018.

McNabb, Tyler Dalton. *Religious Epistemology.* Cambridge: Cambridge University Press, 2018.

McNabb, Tyler Dalton. "Wiley Coyote and the Craggy Rocks Below: The Perils of Godless Ethics." *Philosophia Christi* 20, no. 2 (2018): 339–46.

McNabb, Tyler Dalton and Joseph Blado. "Mary and Fátima: A Modest C-Inductive Argument for Catholicism." *Perichoresis* 18, no. 5 (2020): 55–65.

Meesen, Auguste. "Apparitions and Miracles of the Sun." *International Forum in Porto, Science, Religion, and Conscience.* October 23–25, 2003.

McPherson, David. *Virtue and Meaning: A Neo-Aristotelian Perspective.* Cambridge: Cambridge University Press, 2020.

Mill, John Stuart. *Utilitarianism,* edited by Roger Crisp. Oxford: Oxford University Press, 2004.

Mitchell, Donald W. *Spirituality and Emptiness.* Mahwah: Paulist Press, 1991.

Mitchell, Donald W. *Buddhism: Introducing the Buddhist Experience.* 2nd ed. Oxford: Oxford University Press, 2008.

Mitchell, Donald W., and O.S.B James Wiseman, eds. *The Gethsemani Encounter: A Dialogue on the Spiritual Life by Buddhist and Christian Monastics.* New York: Continuum, 1997.

Mullins, R.T. *God and Emotions.* Cambridge: Cambridge University Press, 2020.

Nagarjuna, Mulamadhyamaka-Karika. *The Fundamentals of the Middle Way,* edited by George Cronk, *Celojumi Talo Austrumu Kulturas,* 1998, http://www.tulkojumi.net/translations/Nagarjuna.%20Madhyamika%20ENG.pdf.

Nagel, Thomas. "What Is It Like to Be a Bat?" *The Philosophical Review* 83, no. 4 (1974): 435–50.

Nishida, Kitaro. *An Inquiry into the Good.* New Haven and London: Yale University Press, 1990.

O'Connor, Timothy. "Simplicity and Creation." *Faith and Philosophy* 16, no. 3 (1999): 405–12.

O'Neill, Andrew. *Tillich: A Guide for the Perplexed.* New York: Continuum Books, 2008.

Oderberg, David S. *Moral Theory: A Non-Consequentialist Approach.* Abingdon, UK: Wiley-Blackwell, 2000.

Paley, William. *The Principles of Moral and Political Philosophy*. Indianapolis: Liberty Fund, 2002.

Pannenberg, Wolfhart. "The Abe-Pannenberg Encounter, Afterword." In *Masao Abe: A Life of Zen Dialogue*, edited by Donald W. Mitchell. Boston: Tutle Publishing, 1998, 208–10.

Pawl, Tim. "Immutability." *Internet Encyclopedia of Philosophy*, https://www.iep.utm.edu/div-immu/

Pinnock, Clark H. *A Wideness in God's Mercy: The Finality of Jesus Christ in a World of Religions*. Grand Rapids, MI: Zondervan, 1992.

Pitre, Brant James. *The Case for Jesus: The Biblical and Historical Evidence for Christ*. New York: Penguin Random House, 2016.

Plantinga, Alvin. *God and Other Minds: A Study of the Rational Justification of Belief in God*. Ithaca: Cornell University Press, 1967.

Plantinga, Alvin. *God, Freedom, and Evil*. Grand Rapids: Eerdmans Publishing Co., 1974.

Plantinga, Alvin. *Does God Have a Nature?* Milwaukee: Marquette University Press, 1980.

Prebish, C. S., and D. Keown. *Introducing Buddhism*. New York and London: Routledge, 2006.

Rea, Michael. *The Hiddenness of God*. Oxford: Oxford University Press, 2018.

Reid, Jasper William. "The Metaphysics of Jonathan Edwards and David Hume." *Hume Studies* 32 (2006): 53–82.

Rettler, Bradley and Andrew Bailey. "Object." *Stanford Encyclopedia of Philosophy*, plato.stanford.edu/entries/object

Rolt, Clarence Edwin. *Dionysius the Areopagite: On the Divine Names and the Mystical Theology*. Grand Rapids: Christian Classics Ethereal Library, 1920, http://www.ccel.org/ccel/rolt/dionysius.html.

Ross, Robert R. N. "The Non-Existence of God: Tillich, Aquinas, and the Pseudo-Dionysius." *The Harvard Theological Review* 68, no. 2 (1975): 141–66.

Ryle, Gilbert. *The Concept of Mind*. Chicago: University of Chicago Press, 1949.

Saṁyutta-nikāya. *Samyutta Nikaya*: The Grouped Discourses. 2009, translated by John T. Bullitt. *Access to Insight*. http://www.accesstoinsight.org/tipitaka/sn/index.html

Sarao, K. T. S. "Vasubandhu," *Internet Encyclopedia of Philosophy*, https://www.iep.utm.edu/vasubandhu/

The Shorter Exhortation to Malunkya Cula Malunkyovada Sutta (MN 63), https://www.dhammatalks.org/suttas/MN/MN63.html

Siderits, Mark. *Buddhism as Philosophy: An Introduction*. Indianapolis: Hackett, 2007.

Solomon, David. "Macintyre and Contemporary Moral Philosophy." In *Alasdair Macintyre*, edited by Mark C. Murphy. Cambridge: Cambridge University Press, 2003, 114–51.

Sullivan, Thomas. "Omniscience, Immutability, and the Divine Mode of Knowing." *Faith and Philosophy* 8, no. 1 (1991): 21–35.

Suzuki, D.T. *Essays in Zen Buddhism, 1st Series*. London: Luzac, 1927.

Suzuki, D.T. *Essays in Zen Buddhism, 2nd Series*. London: Luzac, 1933.

Swinburne, Richard. "What Difference Does God Make to Morality?" In *Is Goodness without God Good Enough?* edited by Robert K Garcia and Nathan L. King. Lanham: Rowman and Littlefield, 2009, 151–66.

Tacitus, Cornelius and N. P. Miller. *Tacitus annals. 15*. London: Bristol Classical Press, 2001.

Talbott, Thomas. *The Inescapable Love of God: Second Edition*. Eugene, OR: Wipf and Stock Publishers, 2014.

Tsering, Geshe Tashi. *Emptiness*. The Foundations of Buddhist Thought. vol. 5. Somerville, MA: Wisdom Publications, Inc., 2018.

Tillich, Paul. *Systematic Theology (Three Volumes)*. Chicago: University of Chicago Press, 1951–1963.

Tomaszewski, Christopher. "Collapsing the Modal Collapse Argument: On and Invalid Argument against Divine Simplicity." *Analysis* 79 (2019): 275–84.

United States Conferences of Catholic Bishops. "What We Believe." http://www.usccb.org/beliefs-and-teachings/what-we-believe/index.cfm

Vallicella, William. "Divine Simplicity." *Internet Encyclopedia of Philosophy*, Plato.Standford.edu/entries/divine-simplicity

Vander Laan, David. "Creation and Conservation." *The Stanford Encyclopedia of Philosophy* (Winter 2017 Edition), edited by Edward N. Zalta, URL = https://plato.stanford.edu/archives/win2017/entries/creation-conservation/.

Von Balthasar, Hans Urs. *Dare We Hope "That All Men Be Saved"?* San Francisco: Ignatius Press, 2014.

Varghese, Roy Abraham. *God-Sent: A History of the Accredited Apparitions of Mary*. New York: Crossroad Pub. Co, 2011.

Walshe, Maurice. *The Long Discourses of the Buddha: A Translation of the Digha Nikaya*. Somerville, MA: Wisdom Publications, 1995.

Westerhoff, Jan. *Nāgārjuna's Madhyamaka: A Philosophical Introduction*. New York: Oxford University Press, 2009.

Westerhoff, Jan. "Metaphysical Issues in Indian Buddhist Thought." In *A Companion to Buddhist Philosophy*, edited by Steven M. Emmanuel. Hoboken, NJ: Wiley-Blackwell, 2013, 129–150.

Wielenberg, Erik J. "Divine Deception." In *Skeptical Theism: New Essays*, edited by Trent Dougherty and Justin P. McBrayer. Oxford: Oxford University Press, 2014, 236–49.

Wilkinson, Robert. *Nishida and Western Philosophy*. Farnham: Ashgate, 2009.

Index

CPSIA information can be obtained
at www.ICGtesting.com
Printed in the USA
LVHW080159150322
713486LV00003B/41

9 781350 189133